PLANNING FOR BILINGUAL LEARNERS
an inclusive curriculum

with best wishes

Maggie.

PLANNING FOR BILINGUAL LEARNERS
an inclusive curriculum

edited by Maggie Gravelle

Trentham Books
Stoke on Trent, UK and Sterling, USA

Trentham Books Limited

Westview House	22883 Quicksilver Drive
734 London Road	Sterling
Oakhill	VA 20166-2012
Stoke on Trent	USA
Staffordshire	
England ST4 5NP	

First published 2000

British Library Cataloguing-in-Publication Data
A catalogue record for this book is available from the British Library

1 85856 175 2

Designed and typeset by Trentham Print Design Ltd., Chester and printed in Great Britain by Cromwell Press Ltd., Wiltshire.

Contents

1
Introduction
Maggie Gravelle

The literature about the practical aspects of teaching bilingual learners is mainly of two kinds. There are useful case studies illustrating the ways in which thoughtful and concerned practitioners have provided opportunities for bilingual learners to succeed in the mainstream. These often identify specific materials and approaches and, sometimes only by implication, display an understanding of the theory and principles informing the practice. I include in this category the general advice to be found in many texts about what to take into consideration when planning for bilingual learners – matters like making sure that their languages are known and respected, and ensuring that dual language texts are included in the book corner.

Alternatively teachers can draw upon a range of literature discussing aspects of theory such as second language acquisition, the backgrounds and origins of different communities or their languages and the nature of bilingualism. Some, but relatively few, of these go on to draw out the practical implications of the theories they expound. Even fewer suggest a systematic framework which will assist teachers in planning effectively and regularly for the needs of bilingual learners in their own classrooms.

And yet it is, in my experience, largely the latter on which teachers want assistance. Their main concerns are about the day-to-day inclusion of bilingual pupils with differing, but continuing, needs and abilities in their curriculum planning. When the specialist materials and packs have been exhausted, or when they do not seem appropriate, teachers show a genuine desire to make their teaching effective for all their pupils and to be given guidance in order to do so.

Second language acquisition; some practical implications

Theories of second language acquisition are not our direct concern here. Teachers want to know what the research can tell them about practice. What do they need to do?

There is widespread agreement about the implications of our understanding of the process of second language acquisition:

- *It is based on and impelled by a desire to communicate.* Children, and indeed adults, learn another language because they need and want to communicate with the people who use that language. This means that in English-medium schools they want access to written and spoken English. They want to understand what their teachers, peers and others in the school and the wider society are saying. They want to communicate and make themselves understood and to do so directly in face-to-face oral communication and through reading and writing.

  Accordingly it is of prime importance that bilingual learners are placed in communicative situations of this nature and given support in their attempts to interact.

- *They must be treated as communicators from the start.* Even infants who have not yet become competent in their first language are considered to have a level of understanding and are constantly placed in interactive situations. Communication is a matter not merely of words but of gesture, actions, facial expression, tone of voice and above all of practical involvement. Early years educators place great emphasis on play as a means of both learning and developing language and part of the importance of this lies in the connection that is created in the child's understanding between what is being done and how it is articulated through language. Similarly, bilingual learners in the later years of school should be actively included in communicative contexts in the classroom and every effort should be made to make the context comprehensible to them and to understand their responses to it.

- *Emphasis should be on meaning rather than form.* If children are to be treated as communicators then the emphasis must be on communication, on making meanings understood, rather than on 'correctness'. It is of little help to the communicative process if it is held up because of the misuse of plurals or the lack of subject/verb agreement, important though these may be in the later stages of language development. The only criterion is understanding.

This means that certainly in the early stages of second language acquisition non-linguistic forms of communication must supplement and complement the linguistic ones. These can take the form of practical activities, pictures and video, outings, role-play and demonstration, as well as the extensive use of first language whenever possible. In later stages there will be greater reliance on alternative linguistic communication, for example re-phrasing, expanding texts for clarification and illustration, using natural repetition and so on.

- *Language learning takes place with and through other learning.* Bilingual children have an entitlement to education and a personal need to continue to develop their conceptual understanding. Learning cannot be placed on hold while language catches up. This is partly because the time is not available. But it also accords with the principles of equality and entitlement which are an important part of our education system. Children's develop - ment does not stand still and if education and the curriculum are worthwhile then they are worthwhile for bilingual as well as monolingual children.

This places great responsibility on teachers to make the learning understandable to bilingual learners right from the start of their education. Once concepts are understood, the vehicle for developing the language skills is in place. There must also be a recognition that bilingual pupils enter schools at many stages in their educational careers. They may be new to English and to the National Curriculum but they are not new to the world. All children draw on a rich and varied range of experiences beyond the school gates.

- *It requires models of natural speech in a range of normal settings.* The total communicative context of the school is only experienced through being part of that context. It cannot be simulated or sanitised through 'situational' language learning techniques. The range of uses of language can never be fully anticipated, nor artificially created. We also know that, useful as some practice and rehearsal may be, there can be no substitute for the 'real thing' – as long as it is adequately supported to make it comprehensible.

Although there may occasionally be times when extra support is best given in a small group situation there can never be a good argument for regular or extended removal of bilingual learners from the regular classroom where normal language and learning activities are taking place. It is there that they will hear a range of models of English being used for all the purposes that are current in the classroom, and indeed in the playground and around the school. It is helpful if this range includes visitors to the school, the headteacher in assembly, visits to the local environment, role-play and other situations. All have potential for not only hearing models of different language use but also for talking and perhaps writing about them.

- *It is extended and developed through exposure to a range of environments and language models.* None of us ever stops learning our language. We develop our skills through the range of new contexts for their use and through the diversity of linguistic experiences to which we are exposed. At times we learn explicitly through direct instruction or the development of our metalinguistic skills. More often the learning is implicit through reading a new work or being involved in a different discourse. All this enriches our language.

So every context has the potential to become a language learning experience. Bilingual learners have the right to exposure to everything that is deemed desirable for monolingual learners. This includes reading. All children are likely to need support in understanding the range of styles in different genres. Information books are written and organised in ways which differ from narrative, lists, instruction manuals, diaries and so on. To make these explicit will help all learners to extend their range and understanding.

- *Learning a language is a creative process that involves making errors and formulating rules.* Infants learning their first language do not do so solely, or even largely, through imitation. Nor is it a process of trial and error. We know that children develop an understanding of the rule system of the language and apply it with increasing accuracy. At times they will over-generalise a rule that they have internalised, so that all past tense utterances, for example, are constructed with '-ed', ignoring for the time being the irregularities of the language. But eventually these irregularities too become part of the rule system, which is not taught, but acquired through use and internal rule generation. Most of the errors that speakers of second and subsequent languages make are due not to interference from the first language but to the construction of what is sometimes referred to as an 'interlanguage'. This operates in much the same way as the experimental framework for first language development and, as users become more proficient, moves more closely towards the target language.

Correcting a child's speech is not only a negative strategy but is also unhelpful and frequently impedes communicative understanding. We know that if children are discouraged from experimenting they will often 'play safe' and use only those terms with which they feel secure. Errors are often signs of progress and growing confidence. Being involved in a variety of language-rich situations is a vital part of the modelling and learning process.

- *It is a risk-taking process so a supportive environment is important.* When we learnt our first language most if us did so in the security of a loving and interactive relationship in which our needs were paramount. Those around us were anxious to understand and to meet our needs and were concerned about our development. On the whole they did not ridicule or humiliate us. We were also surrounded by cultural practices and artefacts that had meaning for us and helped to define our place in the world and our relationship to those around us.

Bilingual children are often in a very different situation in the school environment. Classrooms may not contain familiar artefacts or scripts. Many of their peers and certainly the other adults will already be fluent speakers of English and able to communicate effectively with each other. They understand and will be part of the culture and norms of the school and the classroom and most of them can operate confidently within it. Many bilingual children will be black and may be subjected to racism.

Some of them will come from traumatic or misunderstood backgrounds and be operating under enormous stress, in addition to having to learn and function in a language in which they are not fluent. Teachers need to be sensitive to all these factors and to take active steps to deal with them effectively.

- *It is not a linear process.* As with much other learning, the process of learning a second, and indeed a first, language is messy. Structures which have been encountered and used successfully one day will be misused and misunderstood in a different context or on subsequent days. Vocabulary and forms of language will be forgotten or inadequately internalised and new forms which have not previously been part of the repertoire will suddenly appear.

Since it is *not* a step-by-step process, expecting bilingual learners to retain and use items from one day to the next is unrealistic. Teachers will not be able to tick off the language that has apparently been learnt and leave it as unproblematic.

Research suggests, however, that there is a general order in which language is learnt. Individuals may differ to some extent but, in broad terms, some aspects of language, for example the use of the active present tense, are learnt before others, eg. the passive. Using the simpler forms, together with more complex language, will help early stage learners.

- *Experience of listening is part of language learning.* When we find ourselves in a new linguistic environment many of us need time to 'tune in' long before we become confident enough to contribute. As infants we all spent most of our time listening and then began to make utterances tentatively and briefly before developing our competence more fully. Listening is not necessarily a passive activity.

Teachers are often greatly relieved when they are assured that it is inadvisable to pressurise bilingual learners to talk. But the corollary of this is that they must ensure that the listening can be active, in other words that pupils can make sense of what they are hearing and be given opportunities to participate, whether through speech or other activities.

- *Bilingual learners already have at least one other language to build on.* They all have an understanding of the nature of language and its complexity. For everyone language provides a vital foundation for personal, cultural and social identity and is the method by which we relate to family and friends. Bilingual learners too have done most of their learning up to now through their first language, in which they may also be literate. They use their first language for learning concepts and for learning English. They can test their ideas and develop their understanding using the first language, if possible with other speakers, but inevitably in their thought processes. This ability should be encouraged and seen as an asset. Using two languages is not confusing. For many people it is natural.

Because another language is always available for comparison, bilingual learners often have above average metalinguistic skills. Teachers should build on this and encourage discussion of ways of articulating ideas in both languages. Pupils often welcome explicit linguistic feedback in their acquisition of English, for example through some explanation of how English operates or comparison with their first language.

A Framework for Planning

Theories of second language acquisition can therefore provide helpful guidance about classroom practice. The underlying principles are valuable for long term planning and policy formulation. But for short or medium term planning such theories are still too general.

Bilingual learners have an entitlement to the curriculum and teachers have the responsibility to enable them to learn at whatever stage of English language fluency they enter our schools and classrooms. There are several considerations that teachers need to address in their planning and doing so in a consistent and systematic way will indicate the immediate practical strategies for use with their pupils. Bilingual learners will certainly benefit from this approach to language but none of what is suggested is exclusively for them. Such structures and strategies will help all children to succeed.

When they think about planning and, in particular, differentiation teachers intuitively build on what they know about their pupils. They apply this knowledge to the task to be carried out and consequently devise activities which build on learners' existing knowledge and strengths and provide support for their development.

The framework which follows sets out this process systematically and raises some of the issues of particular relevance to bilingual learners.

A Framework for Planning

	What do learners bring to the task?	What does the task demand of them?	What support needs to be planned?
Social			
Cognitive			
Linguistic			

a) What do learners bring to the task?

We need, firstly, to be aware of what children are bringing to their learning and to the classroom. Children have varied and often detailed knowledge about the world and a range of understandings and explanations for the way it operates.

We need knowledge about all our pupils in terms of their **social** understanding and must be alert to the evidence we use to confirm our knowledge and avoid stereotyping. We have a responsibility to spell and pronounce children's preferred names correctly and to know the names of their parents and family. We need information on the languages that the child uses and their level of literacy in those languages. We should have similar information about the parents so that communication can be effective. Religious observance may entail certain requirements in terms of diet, dress, attendance at assemblies etc. Previous schooling and any supplementary schools attended should also be taken into account. All this must be sensitively collected and documented in the pupil's file.

But there are other aspects of children's social experience that will be specifically relevant to their learning. Are they, for example, familiar with the conventions about teacher/pupil relationships that are a feature of British education? And to the relationships that are the norm in your classroom? Do they feel comfortable about giving opinions or are they more accustomed to being told information? Is the child uncomfortable about sitting on the carpet in close proximity to other children? Do they find movement around the classroom and school a problem? Do children understand when they are expected to raise their hands to speak and when this is not necessary? Are they experiencing natural uncertainties about a new environment and are these compounded by racism? Do children share and collaborate or is more emphasis given to individual achievement?

Our understanding of these issues must be based on sensitively acquired knowledge about the particular child and their circumstances and not on generalisation and stereotyping. We need to ensure that we provide a secure and supportive learning environment for all children.

Eve Gregory (1996) for example, describes the critical attitude of a Hong Kong Chinese family towards the approach to reading of the school their five-year-old attended. For them learning to read was an arduous and formal activity which required above all obedience and accuracy. They regarded 'looking at picture books' without being able to read them as frivolous and time-wasting. Their son brought these expectations with him when first introduced to quiet or shared reading time.

As well as understanding that parental attitudes might differ from those of the school, we need to know what **cognitive** understanding children bring to a particular aspect of the curriculum. Even though they may have had little formal schooling, many bilingual learners will have knowledge of the world far beyond and different from that of their indigenous peers. Many will have travelled, often great distances and several times and might have lived in areas and societies very different from their present one. They will know about other climates, forms of agriculture and industry, fauna and flora, diets and dress.

Much of this knowledge will be relevant across the curriculum. Children whose families have lived and depended on rivers, lakes and seas for their livelihood will understand about aquatic life cycles, floating and sinking, capacity and balance – all from direct experience. Others who have had responsibility for members of the family might know more about the Social Security system, hospitals and doctors and public transport, than many of their peers. And many will have been to schools in other countries, with different curriculums and different sources of information. Some may have different priorities in terms of their learning. The importance of play and creative activities in the British educational system is not universally understood or accepted. Some countries give more emphasis to outdoor and physical activities than we do. Learning and teaching styles also vary. In many countries primary education is more formal than in the UK; in other countries our approach is regarded as rigid and constraining. Standards of behaviour may also differ.

One of the most important skills children bring to their learning is their **linguistic** ability. Simply to know the 'Stage of English language fluency' of the bilingual learners will be of relatively little use at this level of planning. A detailed understanding of ability in all four language areas – speaking, listening, reading and writing – and in languages other than English will need to inform the planning. Bilingual children not only speak at least one language fluently and may also read and write it, they also know how and when to use the appropriate language and constructions. They will, for example, be familiar with the difference between instructions and statements. They may have a grasp of the vocabulary connected with a particular activity in English but not have the confidence to use it in complete sentences.

They may locate some areas of knowledge more securely in English than in their first language. Children who have learnt about electricity in English-medium schools may know the English words for 'crocodile clip' and 'accumulator' but not its counterpart in their first language. Helen Savva (1990) describes Loretta, literate in Armenian, Farsi and English, who switches from Farsi to English when writing about the British history she has learnt at school. On the other hand some foodstuffs, relationships and festivals will be named only, or more appropriately, in first language.

For some children listening and participating in the activities may be sufficient; for others it will be useful to see written English. Many will benefit from the opportunity to talk and perhaps read and write in their first language in order to help their understanding. They will appreciate the need to use English when communicating with those who do not share their first language. For all pupils discussion will increase their understanding. We need to know what contribution bilingual pupils bring to such discussions in order to plan supportive and effective groupings.

b) What does the task demand?

In order to plan effectively we must understand what the task requires of children so that we can plan the support they need on the basis of what we know they can already do. These demands, too, can be analysed in three categories, since all learning involves **social interaction**, cognitive development and linguistic engagement.

Some of the rules in learning tasks are hidden and it can be helpful to make these clear. Are children expected or allowed to talk? Do teachers welcome comments and questions when they are reading aloud? Is the task to be collaborative or individual? Will this apply throughout the activity or is the form of organisation to change at some stage? How is this indicated? Are children to follow directions rigidly or is some autonomy involved? Will materials be handed out or are children expected to collect them? At what stage will teachers and other adults intervene? What are children expected to do if they don't understand or need help? What will happen with the product? If worksheets are used, can they be written on? Are they working documents, rough drafts, or do they replace a text book? How long is the activity expected to take? Will children be asked to share their ideas or their results? Is there a 'right' answer?

To make these matters quite clear is good practice. It helps all children with their learning and will be particularly important for bilingual learners who may not yet have 'picked up' the rules of the classroom. Consistency will be useful, but children also need to learn that there are different behaviours and methods of organisation that are appropriate in different contexts.

Above all, teachers needs to be clear and pro-active about tackling racism. When children refuse or show reluctance to co-operate, make derogatory comments or mistreat each other and their work, these incidents must be dealt with immediately. Teachers have every right to insist on high standards of behaviour and respect in their classrooms and schools. It may be adequate to say that a particular response or behaviour is unacceptable and to deal with it fully later, in order not to interrupt the lesson, but no racist remark or action should go unchallenged. If we do not tackle racism we are giving children a clear message about its acceptability (see Jones, R, 1999).

Equally, if children, and bilingual learners in particular, are to feel secure and respected and if they are encouraged to bring their experiences and understandings of the world into the school, these must be received with attention and sensitivity. Pupils who report racist or other distressing incidents, whether in or outside school, must be treated seriously and given support.

All the training and experience that teachers have equips them to determine the **cognitive** demands of the tasks that they set. While the National Curriculum and other government initiatives will provide the framework, the details of learning need to be carefully analysed. This is particularly important in the case of bilingual learners. Some of the concepts which are part of the background and culture of indigenous pupils may be new to children from other backgrounds. The term 'Victorian' may give rise to images in the minds of British pupils very different from children from the ex-colonies and different again from those who come from countries with few historical links with Britain. On a simpler level the concept of 'bread' and the connotations it carries with it are culturally varied. Pupils from urban backgrounds may have a different understanding to those from rural areas about the source and production of their food, for instance.

Being explicit and reinforcing conceptual references will assist all learners and invite a more enquiring attitude. When dealing with shapes, for example, it helps the less confident pupils to revisit concepts of sides and corners or faces and vertices. This not only reminds all pupils of the concepts but also reinforces the vocabulary which will benefit bilingual learners.

Medium term planning documents, for example the National Numeracy and Literacy Strategies and the QCA curriculum guidance, increasingly specify teaching objectives, but these still have to be analysed and implemented in relation to particular activities and specific learners.

Bilingual pupils are learning English with and through their other learning. The two aspects – language and learning – reinforce each other. Understanding a mathematical operation will enhance understanding of the language associated with it. Learning the language of climatic variation will assist knowledge of meteorology. But in order to support the **language** development of bilingual learners in this context we need to be aware of the difficulties such texts might present, depending on the pupil's existing skills. It is possible, however, to offer general guidelines for teachers who are not necessarily expert linguists and who may agree with the widely held view that all that is needed is for vocabulary to be explained, simplified or translated.

One way of analysing language demands is to look at text, sentence and word level in a manner which mirrors the structure of the National Literacy Strategy. Although bilingual learners are likely to begin using English to produce single word utterances or short phrases, they will be attempting to understand discourse as whole texts, whether spoken or written. So it is important to ensure that pupils can see and hear the text and are given sufficient time to understand it.

Text can be difficult to follow if the cohesive links are not obvious. In spoken language the cohesion can be broken by interruptions. If a teacher switches from giving instructions to admonishing a child or makes an 'aside' while reading a story, this can cause difficulties for bilingual learners unless the switch is marked in some way, for example by gesture or changing intonation and the discourse is repeated or recapped before resuming the flow.

In written language cohesion could be marked by repetition of words or phrases or by repeated reference to particular ideas or objects. There are some styles of writing, however, that deliberately obscure such repetitions by changing the vocabulary.

> In 1492, Caribbean islanders saw Columbus's ships approaching. They thought they came from the sky, home of powerful spirits. Columbus inspired adventurous Europeans from the 'Old World' to visit America, the 'New World'. People from Spain, England, France and Russia came in search of land, minerals and furs. Some tried to convert the tribes to their religion;

others used them as slaves. Europe acquired trade goods and new foods, such as chocolate, sunflowers, corn and peanuts; Native Americans gained guns, horses, metal tools and whisky. Old and New worlds did not mix well. White settlers often took land by force and shot thousands of buffalo for sport. Native Americans, who shared most things and wasted little, could not understand this behaviour. (Thomas and Pendleton,1995)

Here Caribbean islanders are also referred to as 'Native Americans', 'tribes' or by the pronouns 'they' and 'them'. 'Acquired' and 'gained' are used as alternatives in order to vary the vocabulary and improve the style. One repetition that is retained, the use of 'they' in line 2, is confusing in that the two referents are different. The problem is further compounded by the change in subject in the third sentence from 'Caribbean islanders' to 'Columbus' and from then on the narration focuses on Europeans, people from Spain etc. and white settlers, all of whom are the same group.

Cohesion can also be indicated by the use of links such as 'next', 'then', 'meanwhile' and 'however'. These help to identify the structure of the discourse and its purpose. A chronological piece of writing, such as an account or report, and some narratives might well be marked by the use of 'first', 'then', 'later', 'afterwards'. Persuasive text and argument is more likely to feature 'moreover', 'but', 'then again', 'even so'. These words can have quite subtle meanings which are crucial to a grasp of the text as a whole.

The historical text above is written in the active voice. The people are identified with their actions. Much non-fiction is in the passive voice in which things are done to the subjects not by them. For example, 'Europeans were inspired' is passive and this obscures the source of the inspiration. This is often a deliberate de-personalising tool, such as in scientific reports when the experimenters are considered unimportant or are genuinely unknown. But it can also make the text more difficult to understand.

Another possible source of difficulty is the length of the sentences and the nature of the punctuation. The longest sentence in the passage about Columbus has 23 words, divided by a semi-colon. Some texts, often non-fiction, have considerably longer sentences with several subsidiary clauses. But short sentences in themselves do not ensure comprehensibility, in fact simplification removes some of the helpful repetition or explanation. Experienced readers will understand, from other reading and from the punctuation, that the 'Old

World' refers to Europe and 'New World' is America and that Spain, England, France and Russia are part of Europe. But these may offer bilingual learners challenges that are both cognitive and linguistic.

In some non-fiction the layout and design support understanding. Headings and sub-headings as well as pictures, diagrams, maps and charts can give clear indication of the subject matter and the main ideas conveyed. In other cases these can fragment the information. Texts at upper secondary level are often written as continuous prose, with fewer clues to help bilingual learners.

As pupils gain in experience they will encounter and understand a greater range of grammatical structures. The closer written discourse is to speech, the more easily it is understood. But writing has its own conventions and forms of expression and these may be unfamiliar. Spoken language is often grammatically fairly simple, of the subject, verb, object type. But in writing, clauses such as '*who shared most things and wasted little*' (above) make the discourse both more interesting and more complex. Or a sentence may not start with the subject: '*In 1492, Caribbean islanders saw Columbus's ships approaching*'. Or words and phrases may be omitted because the reader is expected to understand the implication as in '*They thought they came from the sky,* (which is the) *home of powerful spirits*'.

The nature of a written text and the relationship between the reader and writer can make it more difficult to follow. Are the *trade goods* and the *new foods* the same or different? Were *sunflowers* used for food? How did Columbus *inspire* Europeans? What was their *religion*? Reading aloud can sometimes clarify meaning, not only because the reader is then available to speak for the writer, but also because intonation can support understanding. 'They are *eating* apples' takes on a different meaning from 'They are eating *apples*.'

Of course vocabulary needs to be intelligible and translation of key words can sometimes be helpful. But most people are conscious of the difficulties of unknown and particularly technical vocabulary and take pains to explain it. Bilingual learners often have greater difficulty with familiar words that are being used in unusual or unfamiliar ways. On the same page the writer talks about the '*hard labour*' brought by the Spanish settlers to the Caribbean and about '*built-in resistance*' to disease. (How does 'built-in' differ from 'in-built'?) These terms might be explained, but would the phrase

'*Native American who* **adopted** *Christianity*'? Many words in English have multiple meanings. A book can be 'by the window', 'by Charles Dickens' or 'by itself on the shelf'. The sole of a shoe is different from the fish called a sole, different again from sole meaning only and from its homophone, soul.

c) What support needs to be planned?

Analysing the demands of the activity and matching them with what the pupils already know and can do is an essential precursor to planning how the ideas and skills are to be taught and what support needs to be incorporated.

Support may be needed for the social and cognitive as well as linguistic demands and can take many forms. **Social** demands are often met by determining which groups bilingual learners are to work in and how to make these truly collaborative so that all participants can and do contribute. This requires that teachers plan for the role bilingual learners are to take. Even if their English language skills are still limited, pupils will be able to participate in practical activities and in some of the decision-making involved, even if only by agreeing or disagreeing. For many bilingual learners their receptive understanding is in advance of their ability to produce language, and their oral skills more developed than their literacy. Children need the opportunity to talk through their ideas in a supportive group situation in order to increase their confidence as well as their understanding.

The optimal size and composition of the groups will depend on the activity and on the skills and needs of the pupils so the groups will not remain fixed. For some tasks pairs are recommended and these may often be of pupils who share a first language but for others larger groups of mixed linguistic skills will encourage development of English alongside understanding of the task.

Grouping together pupils who share a first language can accelerate learning, particularly in the case of new arrivals. Some teachers identify particular partners to become 'friends' or 'buddies' with recent arrivals for learning purposes. Regular feedback between teachers and the friendship pairs can help to establish what learning has taken place and what other strategies and resources would be supportive. Such partnerships have been found rewarding for pupils with greater fluency in English as well as for new arrivals.

As already suggested, the organisation of any task and the expected outcomes should be made clear to all learners. This will help remove uncertainty and put bilingual children at their ease. Any other measures that might reduce stress should also be considered. Familiar resources, reflecting the children's own backgrounds and experiences will be helpful. But most of all it is important to establish an ethos of acceptance and of sharing, in which racism and discrimination are identified but not tolerated. Such an atmosphere is also likely to promote speculation and hypothesising; pupils will try out new ideas in the knowledge that they will be respected.

The nature and extent of support for **cognitive** development will depend on the children's existing skills and knowledge. Many of the teaching strategies are already part of teachers' repertoire. Gesture, intonation and facial expression can aid understanding, as can observing or engaging in role-play. Sometimes additional explanation, using varied examples or vocabulary can clarify matters. Visual support is often useful and care should be exercised in selecting positive and varied pictures, videos, charts and diagrams. Similarly 'realia' or artefacts can make an activity come alive and provide links with children's experiences.

Offering examples and models of the process and outcome of the activity is an important strategy. Teachers are accustomed to showing children the stages they might go through when making a map, cooking pizza or designing a robot. Even when there are a variety of ways of approaching a task which is intended to remain open-ended, some guidance is likely to be helpful. But teachers also need to remain flexible and resist giving the impression that any single example or explanation is the only correct or possible one.

Sharing and summarising learning at the end of a lesson or session is also extremely supportive. Doing so shows learners the range of achievements within the class and provides them with opportunities to demonstrate their individual and group attainment. It is a way for the teacher to reinforce the learning outcomes and to discuss the processes involved. Sensitive teachers will treat all contributions positively, using praise and encouragement to include bilingual learners in the plenary. This also provides excellent opportunity for teachers to assess real learning, much of which may be unexpected. Teachers who are open and flexible will encourage children to discover learning in many different areas.

Linguistic development goes hand in hand with cognitive progression. By making activities linguistically accessible one is increasing children's conceptual understanding. Many of the ways of doing this are part of normal classroom practice. When pupils talk and explore ideas together they are practising and perhaps extending their linguistic skills. They are also laying a good foundation for literacy. Talking about books helps to remind us of their content and organisation as well as to evaluate and relate them to our lives and to other texts. Discussing an activity can lead to a writing task. It is important that such talk has a clear structure and purpose and should frequently be in the first language of the bilingual pupils. Such discussion gives learners a valuable opportunity to rehearse their skills in a small group situation.

Working in isolation is almost always more demanding than working collaboratively. Group writing, where the confident writers, teacher or another adult do the scribing, leaves other pupils free to contribute and discuss ideas orally. This provides a supportive environment for bilingual learners and also a model of a particular type of writing. But there are times when children prefer to explore and develop their own ideas in writing and to keep a personal record of their thoughts or events.

One way we learn and refine our language skills is by seeing and hearing a range of discourse. So providing models is an effective way of supporting linguistic development. It indicates to pupils what they should be aiming for and clarifies the teacher's expectations in a concrete way that cannot be achieved just by explanation. As children become increasingly confident with the form, they can adapt and transform it to their own uses and are often very creative. Some of pupils' failures are due to their uncertainty about what is required.

The National Literacy Strategy is part of a growing awareness that explicit exploration and discussion of language is beneficial. Children are interested in finding out about languages, their own and other people's, and investigating ways in which words are used to convey meaning. Bilingual children have greater metalinguistic awareness by virtue of having at least two languages to compare and they can participate in, contribute to and benefit from such sessions. Many of them, particularly if they are beyond the early stages of education, will expect grammatical explanations. If grammar is seen as an exploration of language in use rather than a set of rules to be taught and memorised, this sort of feedback is of benefit.

Many teachers will be familiar with ways of deconstructing and re-constructing discourse to highlight its structure and meaning. DARTs (Directed Activities Related to Text) and Writing Frames are such strategies. Both are ways of exposing the 'bare bones' or struc-ture of a text so that learners can then supply the content and detail. They include sequencing and re-ordering activities, matching sen-tence starts and endings, completing sentences or paragraphs and identifying cohesive links through linking pronouns to the nouns to which they refer, as well as many other techniques.

Phrasing ideas in alternative ways can clarify them. We support pupils when we extend and explain the discourse, whether written or spoken and this is even more effective if first language can also be used. There are times when repetition is more helpful than re-phrasing, principally in the early stages of language acquisition. Certain activities, such as some science experiments or maths activi-ties and many forms of games, invite natural repetition which can be exploited to reinforce language.

Summary

Examining all these aspects of a lesson will help teachers to identify the support that is needed for understanding based on a clear know-ledge of the children's needs and abilities in relation to the tasks they are to undertake. Teachers use the National Curriculum and other documents, along with their own schemes of work to plan their teaching. They already have clear ideas about what they want chil-dren to do in order to achieve particular learning objectives and they are accustomed to articulating these objectives in terms of know-ledge, skills and understanding but less usually in terms of the atti-tudes that they intend to foster. Increasingly classes include bilingual children whose needs are perceived to be different from those of the indigenous pupils. What the framework illustrates is that although these learners may require intervening support in order to gain access to the curriculum, the nature of that support is no different from nor detrimental to the learning of all children.

During and after a session, teachers monitor and assess children's achievements and evaluate the teaching process. They may discover that some of the children appear to have misunderstood a concept and need to re-visit it in a different form or that they have higher level skills than anticipated. They may decide that a particular pair worked well together or that the way they introduced a certain idea requires further exemplification. All this provides new sources of information on which to base future planning. So the whole process becomes cyclical, with more and more information being accumulated about individual children and growing experience of meeting their needs.

This level of analysis is part of the professional approach of all teachers, although many do it intuitively rather than explicitly. It is necessary for the effective learning of all pupils and certainly for all bilingual pupils – not just beginners in English, whose needs are identifiable to all, but also those whose apparent oral fluency makes support seem less necessary. It is the learners who appear to manage in the classroom but whose achievement is in fact depressed because their linguistic needs are not appreciated, that are of particular concern.

Primary classrooms, where all children are developing their language skills alongside their other learning and where teachers have the experience and organisation to meet these needs, are often assumed to be more conducive to language acquisition than secondary classrooms. Focused attention is certainly beneficial in the early years, but classrooms remain demanding places for bilingual pupils of all ages. Teachers of all subjects and in all Key Stages have a responsibility to consider ways of making their curriculum accessible and relevant to all pupils.

Outline of the book

The chapters that follow provide real and vivid examples of the nature of the planning process and of the strategies that have been used to support the learning and language development of bilingual pupils. Examples have been drawn from different subject areas and different Key Stages. The contexts within which the pupils are learning also differ – from a primary school with very few bilingual learners and limited specialist support, to a large, multi-ethnic secondary school with a team of experienced teachers who collaborate with mainstream colleagues to ensure curriculum access for all.

In chapter 2 Elaine Sturman describes how she used a story to extend children's thinking and reasoning while providing carefully planned support for their language development. Richard Gifford, in chapter 3, describes the progress made by one bilingual child and the opportunities that her presence provided for teachers and pupils to gain confidence in meeting her needs. The book *Mufaro's Beautiful Daughters*, discussed in chapter 4, was used in the Literacy Hour to promote and value the use of first language, and this theme is developed in chapter 5 by Zaitun Virani-Roper in her discussion of the effective inclusion of bilingual learners in the Numeracy Hour. Steve Cooke and Susan Pike describe in chapter 6 the detailed planning that took place in a Geography lesson with Year 9 and how they used key visuals as one of the strategies to support learning and facilitate planning. The use of key visuals is a feature of the work that Dympna MacGahern and Kwaku Boaten, part of a team of language support teachers in a large secondary school, describe in chapter 7. They illustrate the importance of planning jointly with mainstream colleagues in a number of curriculum areas. Finally, in chapter 8, Claire Edmunds discusses the principles behind an understanding of language development and the importance of formal and informal training in building teachers' confidence.

A note on terminology

The 1966 Local Government Act which provided money for the support of certain groups of ethnic minority learners under Section 11 has been superseded in April 1999 by the Ethnic Minority Achievement Grant (EMAG), since renamed Ethnic Minority and Traveller Achievement Grant (EMTAG). Most of this grant, which comes from the DfEE, is devolved directly to schools to 'support activity specifically designed to improve the attainment of minority ethnic, Traveller and refugee pupils in particular' (Standards Fund, Sept. 1999). Some schools have set up, or retained, specialist teams to offer such support. Others have been able to employ individual teachers, sometimes managed by the Special Needs Co-ordinator, to fulfil this role. In other cases the LEA, who are entitled to retain 15% of the funding, have continued to employ an Ethnic Minority Achievement Service, or similar, to provide a central advisory team and peripatetic teachers for bilingual learners. Local authorities remain responsible for monitoring the effective use of grant monies.

Much of the current literature, including documents from the QCA and the DfEE, use the term English as an Additional Language (EAL) to refer to pupils whose first language is other than English. It is interesting that in many cases the only language that is considered to be of importance is English and the first, home, or heritage language(s) to which English is additional are ignored. While it seems to me perfectly proper to refer to the teaching of English as an Additional Language by the use of an acronym it is demeaning to discuss pupils and teachers as EALs. In general the term *bilingual* is used in this book, although it is often inaccurate since many people speak more than two languages and should properly be referred to as multilingual. A further objection is that pupils with extremely limited English should be considered as monolingual until such time as they reach a certain degree of fluency. The term bilingual is therefore used with these reservations, as a general description of those who have access to more than one language in their daily lives. It is not intended to give any indication of the levels of fluency in any language, nor of the range or extent of language use.

Resources
Thomas, D and Pendleton, L (1995) *Native Americans*, Macdonald Young Books.

2

Jamaica's Find: using a story book
to develop ideas about writing
Elaine Sturman

Pupils should be able to:
demonstrate, in talking about stories and poems, that they are beginning to
use inference, deduction and previous reading experience to find and appreciate meanings beyond the literal. (*English in the National Curriculum: Reading 1989*, 3d)

When this version of the English National Curriculum was published, I was teaching a Year 2 class and this statement made a particular impression on me. There was a related statement in Attainment Target 3, encouraging children to write 'Stories which include a description of setting and the feelings of characters.' Was I noticing these elements in my children's writing?

All the children in my class were bilingual. Most of them had been in the school since the nursery and were fluent users of English. I had thought that their reading and writing skills were developing satisfactorily, but then realised that I had not concentrated specifically on the elements of reading and particularly writing highlighted in these statements.

I had often heard the argument that bilingual children, although capable of writing well-structured and detailed factual accounts, found it difficult to produce something more imaginative. Some teachers seemed to feel that this difficulty was directly related to bilingualism. I always maintained that the reason children were not producing imaginative writing was more likely to be because they had not been given sufficient opportunities to consider and analyse how such writing is constructed. Using popular story books, I had worked with children on making charts of the story structure, comparing characters and writing sequels. I had found that talk and discussion supported by a defined task helped to clarify and refine the writing demands. I now needed to find a story which would support reading about, discussing and finally writing about a character's feelings.

The book I chose was *Jamaica's Find*. It is set in surroundings which would be familiar to all children – the local park, the family home – and takes place in a framework which all could relate to – family relationships, friendship. Most importantly, the story raises a moral dilemma and provides an opportunity to explore Jamaica's feelings about the course of action she decides to take.

I prefer to start any activities around a book by reading the story to the children. For me, and I hope for the children, this is always an enjoyable joint experience. During the reading, I can check the children's understanding and note any initial comments and reactions. Reading the book aloud was particularly important for *Jamaica's Find*. Although the story is written in straightforward language with plenty of dialogue, the length, range of vocabulary and complexity of sentence structure would make the book a daunting read for some six year-olds. Familiarity with the context, and the illustrations that complement the text so well, would support the children's understanding as they listened to the story.

I devised a series of activities based on the book that would promote discussion and lead into a writing task. The activities gave children the opportunity to work as a whole class and in pairs before moving on to individual writing, and encouraged plenty of discussion and collaboration, essential for understanding and development.

The Activities
Whole class: reading

The story lends itself to a prediction activity, which was likely to be particularly successful in my class as none of the children knew the book. I started to read, showing the pictures to aid their understanding, but without comment.

On her way home for tea, Jamaica stops in the park to play. She finds a woolly hat and a rather bedraggled toy dog underneath the slide. She takes the hat to the lost property office but keeps the dog and takes it home. Her family express reservations, gently pointing out that she should have given the dog to the lost property office and that it is not very clean. Jamaica takes the dog to her room and throws it on a chair. There is a picture of her sitting on the bed contemplating the dog.

At this point I stopped reading and asked the children to retell the story so I could be sure that they had understood the main points and to provide reinforcement for any child who needed it.

Whole class: brainstorm

Brainstorming is a useful way of exploring issues, gathering a range of responses and tuning in to children's ideas and understandings. It is only successful if everyone is clear that all responses will be accepted without challenge or contradiction. This can be quite difficult to establish, as children are used to trying to find answers in the teacher's head and teachers are often tempted to intervene to refine or re-present a suggestion. The first attempt at brainstorming may be disappointing, with perhaps only a few children participating and the teacher having to play too large a part, but it is worth persevering. Once the technique is familiar, children will become secure enough to express their views. Although it is possible to have a purely oral brainstorm, I have found it more useful to scribe responses for children to see. Apart from providing an added reading experience and a written record of what has been said, it also gives an opportunity for language development. Discussing with children how to record their ideas reveals the differences between spoken and written language and helps children to rehearse and compare the two forms.

For this brainstorm I showed children the picture of Jamaica sitting on her bed looking rather grimly at the dog, but did not read the accompanying text. It might be helpful to enlarge this picture and have it on display to remind children of the stimulus for their ideas. I invited the children to suggest what Jamaica might decide to do and recorded all their suggestions on a flip chart.

These were some of the suggestions:

wash the dog

keep the dog

put the dog back where she found it

take the dog back to the Lost Property office

take the dog to school (to see if it belongs to any of her friends)

go around the houses trying to find the owner

make posters advertising that the dog has been found

put the posters on lamp-posts

put an advert in the paper .... or on local radio

take the dog to the shop and swap it for a new one

I was pleased with the outcome of the brainstorm. Although they started rather tentatively, the children soon became animated, picking up and expanding each other's suggestions. I was surprised that washing the dog was one of the first ideas and had wide approval. I had hardly registered that the dog was dirty, but to the children this was important and required attention. We now had an interesting range of suggestions which could be expanded in the next activity.

Pair work: planning sheet

To encourage the children to think about emotions, they explored how Jamaica might feel if she adopted some of the brainstorm suggestions. As there was scope for different points of view, I asked children to work in pairs and give their own opinions. They would have to explain and justify their view to a partner and try to reach a shared position. To support the discussion each pair was given a worksheet divided into three columns with the headings:

Jamaica could...	Good or bad	How would she feel?

The worksheet was divided into four horizontal sections. In the first column, pairs wrote four possible actions chosen from the brainstorm suggestions or their own ideas. Then they decided whether the action would be good or bad and how Jamaica would feel if she took that course. Although the main point of the activity is the discussion and decision-making there is the possibility for vocabulary development on adjectives which describe feelings. Introductory shared work on adjectives for positive and negative feelings helps encourage children to use a wider vocabulary than simply 'happy' or 'sad' in the final column.

Jamaica	Good/bad	Feels
give the dog To the lost propaty office	good	Sad
Keep The dog	Bad	Happy
buy a dog	good	Happy
take The dog Back To The Park	good	Sad

If children are not used to working in pairs they may find it difficult at first to collaborate. As each pair has only one worksheet, practical decisions about how the writing is shared will be important. The reading and writing is not very demanding at this stage – the first column can be copied from the flip chart and one word answers (good, bad, happy, sad) or even happy and sad faces are adequate for the second and third columns. So it is not necessary to make sure that each pair has a competent reader and writer. If discussing and reaching consensus are new to the children it will probably help if they work with a classmate with whom they feel comfortable and relaxed.

Children in my class tackled the worksheet with gusto. Not all pairs completed the four sections, but all managed at least one horizontal line. Not all pairs agreed on whether the action was good or bad, but they found ways of resolving their differences (alternating each child's view, abandoning a first column on which they disagreed, including both views with justification). Not all pairs extended the third column beyond 'happy' and 'sad' but all discussed how Jamaica would feel in each situation. I think the activity worked because it followed directly from something in which they had all been involved and extended it in ways that made sense without being too demanding in terms of reading and writing.

At the end of the session, I asked each pair to choose one horizontal line from their sheet to share with the whole class.

Whole class: plenary

As I had expected, interesting issues for discussion emerged when children expressed their opinions that a 'good' action resulted in Jamaica feeling bad and a 'bad' action, such as taking the dog made her, at first, feel happy. We wondered how this could be? Shouldn't 'good' actions always make us happy and can we be happy if we do something we feel is not right? Children may start to express more complex emotional responses ('a bit happy, a bit sad', as one of my pairs wrote). Such dilemmas are an essential concern of literature but there is also a strong cross-curricular link with PSHE.

Once children are beginning to talk about complex emotions, they can be encouraged to think of how to express this in writing. One way is by choosing an appropriate adjective. A class list of adjectives expressing feelings could be compiled using examples from the plenary. Some of the adjectives my class suggested were:

excited   embarrassed

upset   heartbroken

Finding adjectives expressing emotion in the books they are reading, and talking about how and when these are used will help to give children confidence to introduce this vocabulary into their own writing.

Story writing

The children now appeared ready to move on to extended writing. They were asked to develop one of the lines from their pair work to construct a possible ending to Jamaica's story

Preparing for story writing is always difficult as there are so many factors to be considered: starting point, setting, coherence, language, grammar, punctuation, spelling – the list is daunting. For this task I emphasised that the story should build on previous work by expanding the course of action and describing how Jamaica felt. To reinforce this, I reminded children that the starting point for the story was the point we had reached in the book where Jamaica was sitting on her bed thinking. They remembered that it was evening and Jamaica was at home. I told them that as I read their stories I would be looking specifically at their descriptions of Jamaica's feelings. We reviewed the adjectives they might use. We also discussed other ways in which Jamaica's feelings might be conveyed – for example, how she looked, how she behaved.

The children worked in a range of groupings, offering different support:

- Individual – children who felt confident to compose their own story, building on their pair work and the group and class discussion.

- Pair/small group – children who wanted to work together to compose a joint story using their own resources.

- Shared writing – a group session where I scribed the story from the suggestions of children who were not yet confident writers.

The preparation for writing seemed to be adequate, as the children wrote enthusiastically and confidently. They offered new responses to how the situation might be resolved:

> ... She went to sleep she had a drem and it was all abot wot hepet to Jamaica today and she was very sad becase her morder said give the dog bake to the Lost Propt Man ...

> (She went to sleep. She had a dream and it was all about what happened to Jamaica today and she was very sad because her mother said give the dog back to the lost property man)

and finding ways to describe mixed emotions:

> and she weked sade home But she was plesed wet her self.
> (and she walked sadly home. But she was pleased with herself.)

Analysing the writing

Later, I worked on these activities with a Year 3 class in the autumn term where children all completed individual endings to Jamaica's story. I took their writing away to see if any patterns emerged and this proved to be useful in two ways. Firstly, I was able to report back to the children about the content of their work, using real examples from their writing (for example good ideas for resolving Jamaica's dilemma, imaginative use of vocabulary to describe feelings). Secondly, I was able to identify the children who would benefit from specific work on aspects of presentation (use of full stops, punctuation of direct speech etc.)

Whole class: reading

I rounded off the work by returning to the book and reading the ending of the story as written by Juanita Havill. In an attempt to pre-empt any feelings that this was the 'right' or definitive ending, I talked to the children about how authors make choices when deciding on plot development. The important thing is not so much what happens as that the events should seem believable and create an atmosphere which the reader can respond to.

In the book, Jamaica feels bad about keeping the dog and, with the strong but silent support of her mother, decides to return it to the lost property office. She is worried about meeting the lost property man again, but feels better when she meets a girl of about her age who is looking under the slide for a lost toy. Jamaica takes the girl to the lost property office and there is a picture of them both smiling happily.

On subsequent readings I asked children to listen for ways in which the author describes how Jamaica feels. There are several examples, both explicit and implicit:

'I feel horrid.' (to her mother when she still has the dog)

feeling hot around her ears (when the lost property man recognises her)

She didn't feel like playing alone (after returning the dog)

Jamaica couldn't keep from shouting (when she realises she has found the owner)

she smiled her biggest smile (returning to the lost property office with the owner)

Jamaica was almost as happy as Kristin (when Kristin has the dog)

Reading development

The activities on *Jamaica's Find* gave children great enthusiasm for the book. Most children were keen to read the story for themselves, even those who would have thought the text too demanding before doing the activities. At this stage it was useful to have multiple copies of the book available for use in shared reading sessions.

Using the activities to support children new to English

I designed these activities for a class of bilingual children, all of whom were fairly fluent in English. I have since used the activities in different classes and found that they have enabled children with little experience of English to participate. I think this is because the activities:

- were based on a familiar situation in a book with strong visual support

- allowed children to listen and see talk represented in writing without putting them under pressure to contribute

- did not expect 'right' answers

- offered possibilities of participation at different levels

- were flexible enough to be adapted according to the needs of the class

Examples of participation from children new to English
Brainstorm

When I used the activities in another Y2 class where the children had little experience of English, I used the flip chart record of brainstormed suggestions to check and reinforce word recognition. I asked children to identity and find examples of particular words which appeared several times. A boy who had only been in school for a week was delighted to be able to take part in this activity by pointing to the word 'on' in various places for other children to read.

Planning Worksheet

During the brainstorm children who are new to English but keen to contribute may need a lot of support from the teacher to re-form their suggestions into an acceptable written form. The repetition and negotiation involved in reaching a written version which represents their meaning and also makes sense to them provides valuable language reinforcement. One Year 3 girl's security in reading the written version of her own suggestion gave her the confidence to read and select other suggestions from the flip chart to record on her planning sheet.

One boy who had previously found writing in English too daunting was determined to record his own suggestion, which I had written on the flip chart, and he managed this with the help of his partner.

Individual writing

A Year 3 boy who was new to the country had completed previous activities with the support of a partner who shared his first language and was also fluent in English. When it came to the writing task, she naturally wanted to work on her own. Undeterred, he drew a dog and a tree, representing the suggestion that Jamaica could make posters to advertise having found the dog. With my support he wrote 'dog found in park'. He then drew Jamaica with a happy smile, insisting on checking with the cover of the book to make sure that he had drawn her hairstyle correctly. His understanding of the task was unmistakable.

Conclusion

This account has tried to show how learning intentions can be put into practice. The National Curriculum is clear about what should be taught and there are plenty of published schemes which give practical suggestions for classroom work. However it is not always clear how the 'what to do' elements fulfil the 'what to teach' requirements. I hope that this work makes that link by:

- having a clear aim (developing writing to include a character's feelings)

- using a supportive framework (a picture book with a familiar setting)

- building in plenty of steps to support the writing (whole class and pair discussion; a defined story line; discussion of appropriate vocabulary)

- making explicit links between reading and writing

My first assessment of the activities related to the fulfilment of my aim, but I also felt children had been given the opportunity to:

- understand how authors develop plot

- explore a moral dilemma and think about the complexity of emotions associated with it

I was also pleased to note the enthusiasm for writing when the preparation is right, and the boost to reading which text-based activities give.

As I have always taught classes which included bilingual learners, I have devised activities with their needs in mind. This does not mean that the activities are particularly, or only, suitable for bilingual children. What it does mean is that I am providing support at every stage and not taking children's previous knowledge and understanding for granted. Where this approach is successful, the activities produced will be eminently suitable for all children. In fact I have recently learned that my work on *Jamaica's Find* is being used successfully in a Surrey school with no bilingual learners.

Resources

Havill, J (1987) *Jamaica's Find*, Mammoth

3
Building confidence for a new arrival – and her teachers
Richard Gifford

Teachers who are unaccustomed to working with beginner bilinguals sometimes find the prospect rather daunting. They may even see it as the last straw at busy times, and are there any times in the school year that aren't busy?

> 'I've got short, medium and long term planning, differentiation, special needs, the literacy and numeracy strategies, my subject co-ordination role, SATs and Ofsted to think about, so how am I going to find the time to cater for the needs of a new arrival without any English?'

The concerns of mainstream teachers about inclusion were considered in the introduction. The first responsibility of any teacher is to provide a safe and welcoming classroom climate for any new arrival, and an ethos which celebrates diversity. Language acquisition is rooted in everyday interactions and a planned framework shows pupils and teachers how this can enable them to participate and benefit from working with other pupils. The point is also made that provision for the bilingual pupil must be *sustainable*; induction of the new arrival is important but it is what goes on in the classroom in the months that follow that will determine whether the bilingual learner will succeed in their new environment.

This chapter charts the progress of a Year 3 Spanish-speaking girl, Pilar, newly arrived in this country from Chile. I followed a pragmatic and flexible approach, based on planning for language acquisition across the curriculum but including frequent changes of plan in response to her progress within the mainstream framework.

Many of the points made in the introduction to this book are strongly illustrated by Pilar's experience. Pilar's desire to communicate in the mainstream has fuelled her progress from the outset. She has developed her speaking and writing from the listening and reading she has done in contextualised situations. She has taken risks and made mistakes but has proved a relaxed and willing learner in response to the encouragement she has received. But her progress has been non-linear. Examples from her work show how much ground she has covered but also that progress has been forward, static or backward at particular times and in particular areas.

Looking back after six months, I still consider the most important factors contributing to her success to be her own motivation, self-esteem and willingness to take risks. She is prepared to speak to the whole class, even to the whole school and, at work or play, is to be found in a happy group of friends. Sometimes the novelty wears off; a new arrival ceases to be interesting to her classmates and she may still be unwilling to expose her emerging proficiency in English to public view. Pilar must take much of the credit herself, but she couldn't have done it without the ethos established by the class teacher and the school as a whole. From the start her teacher provided a positive role model, along the lines of:

> 'You are an ordinary pupil, your Spanish is like your classmates' English, you have knowledge and perspectives to bring into this class, and we will give you time and space to contribute on your terms. You're not a novelty or an exhibit, you're just as ordinary and as special as each of us.'

I had not worked in Pilar's school as a support teacher before she arrived, and its past experience of bilingual pupils was mainly with children from settled Asian communities. She was the only bilingual pupil with whom I worked in the school at the time. At first I made several short visits each week while Pilar was getting settled. These visits settled to two hour-long sessions each week. Pilar was also supported by a Learning Support Assistant from the school and I tried to ensure that I met with her and other staff briefly on each occasion. I only withdrew Pilar from sessions when the style of the lesson was not conducive to in-class support. Usually I worked with her and a small group in the class, encouraging them to listen and talk rather than solely producing written work.

2nd Jan Pilar arrived in January. My first task was to meet her and her mother and to introduce myself to the school, which was not used to beginner bilinguals. I suggested a few starting points. In the early stages it is vital to help create a welcoming atmosphere for the new pupil and to reassure the teacher, so that tensions and anxiety don't build up. Mainstream teachers are often tempted, for well-intentioned but misguided reasons, to isolate the new arrival from other members of the class. They might do this by assigning a heavy dose of 1.1 support from a Learning Support Assistant, gathering up some literacy materials suited to younger children, or setting up some visual computer activities. Bilingual children start to acquire their additional language in the same way they acquired their first language, by **hearing** it in context. So Pilar needed plenty of opportunities to listen and interact.

The first week was about pastoral aims. Pilar needed time to adjust to her new environment, but it was important to get the atmosphere right from the start. I talked to the rest of the class about how Pilar might feel and what sort of help they could give. I encouraged them to be curious about Spanish and Chile, but was ready to intervene if they overstepped the mark. There were times when Pilar found the attention of her peers overwhelming and appreciated the opportunity to melt into the background again. She often found closed questions easier to answer than open-ended ones and I was able to rephrase children's enquiries to enable Pilar to respond. It's quite hard for seven year olds to get the balance right! The mainstream teacher found Pilar a buddy who would show her round and help her with school routines.

To help Pilar establish contact with a few classmates, I withdrew her with a small group for about half an hour and taught them a simple Lotto game, which I call Tap-Tap. She was soon able to help the others to learn and develop the game. The main objective was to get Pilar and the other children talking. Any informal, practical activity would have done; the main point was for me to model for the classmates that it is perfectly possible to communicate with a beginner without resorting to one of the comedy routines the English are prone to fall into.

Pilar knew very few words and had difficulty pronouncing unfamiliar sounds such as 's' and 'b', which became 'th' and 'v' respectively. I was delighted to see that despite this she was prepared to speak to the children. Had she not, I would have switched to a game in which she had only to listen at this early stage, remembering that many beginner bilinguals go through quite a long 'silent period' in which they listen to English but are not ready to start speaking it for themselves.

During the first week I made frequent short visits to Pilar's class, helping her to acclimatise to her new environment and helping the

Tap Tap (based on Lotto)

You need a set of pictures of everyday objects as individual cards and sets (one for each player) that enable players to collect the pictures and thereby cover their card.

Each player has a collecting card and the object is to cover the whole card with matching pictures.

Spread the individual pictures out face up.

The first player tries to name one of the objects s/he wants. If you can name the object you keep the picture. If you can't you point to it and say 'tap tap'. You are then told the name by another player, practise saying it and then you have to remember it until your next turn. The catch is, no-one uses their first language, so in this case Pilar had to use English and the English speakers had to use Spanish! This balances up the players and helps the English pupils to share the feeling of working in a new language.

The game can be developed from single words to phrases such as 'pass me the scissors, please' or 'where is the..?' 'here is the ...' etc. It can be made into a more elaborate memory game by playing with the cards upside down and players take it in turns to turn a card over. If it's one of the ones they want for their card, they try to name the object, or ask another player for the name to learn. Then they turn the card face down again and have to remember the position of the card they want and its name in their new language.

Another variant is playing the game Lotto style. One player can call out the objects one at a time and the others ask for it if it's on their card. Here the bilingual pupil is listening only, not speaking English.

rest of the class to adapt to her. I encouraged Pilar to join in activities such as PE and watching television with the class. Some teachers see such times as appropriate to withdraw the pupil for intensive 1:1 time with perhaps an LSA but these are important opportunities for listening. We need to remember that someone in a new language environment quickly adjusts to being unable to understand everything. Very soon she was able to pick up what she could understand from the unintelligible background, a skill which she continues to use. This is part of the natural process of language acquisition, in which the learner learns to understand the gist of their target language from known key words, then gradually gains a larger vocabulary and syntactic knowledge to enable her to deduce deeper meaning.

I also noticed that at times Pilar was very tired. This is common. A combination of the stress of adapting to a new environment and operating in an unfamiliar language is draining and it is important to give the new arrival time to relax. On occasions during this first period, we encouraged Pilar to write in Spanish. She appeared to have age-appropriate levels of literacy in Spanish and wrote with confidence. It was not possible at this stage to assess her written Spanish formally, nor did I attempt to develop her literacy skills, although a number of bilingual English/Spanish stories were available in the school. I used her writing in Spanish as a vehicle to express her understanding and experiences. This is particularly appropriate for tasks such as writing about a first-hand experience such as a piece of practical science. It must be extremely frustrating to be unable to relate one's cognitive understanding because of restricted language. Time spent working in first language can help to release this tension and also sends important messages to classmates about the bilingual learner's capabilities.

9th Jan Pilar's progress with writing is interesting. She forms letters very poorly in English but writes beautiful cursive script in Spanish. She doesn't seem to have made the connection that the letters are nearly all the same! I worked hard on 'c' and 'a' but she resisted! I talked to her Mum about this and hoped she could explain for me.

11th Jan I left a copy of *Las aventuras de Connie y Diego/The adventures of Connie and Diego*, a dual-language text by Maria Garcia, (Children's Book Press, San Francisco) for her to read at home. We read a little together; she preferred reading to me in English. Pilar knew

We used a list of useful Spanish phrases:

English/Spanish everyday teacher/pupil phrases

Good morning/ afternoon Mr.../ everyone Buenos diás/ tardes senor/ toda la genta.

How are you?	Como estás?
How are things?	Que tal?
Have you finished?	Has terminado?
Good work	Bueno trabajo
Very good	Muy bien
Carefully please	Más exacto por favor
Read your book	Lees tu libro
Write in your book/paper	Escribes en tu cuanderno/papel
Put your book away	Pones el libro en sitro
Do you understand?	Entiendes?
Show me	Muéstera me
Get changed for PE	Cambia los vestidos para haces PE
Homework	Deberes
Spellings	Ortografia
Listen to me	Escucha me
Look	Mira
Draw	Dibujar
Pencil (crayon)	Lápiz (de color)
Cut	Corta
Stand	Lévantage
Sit	Siéntase

that I did not speak Spanish and recognised English as the language of the school, but she may have derived some understanding from reading the Spanish text.

14th Jan I introduced Oxford Reading Tree Stage 2. I like using Reading Tree books with bilingual pupils; they help to build a sight vocabulary with their repetition of high frequency words; the pictures cue the text well and there is an unselfconscious multicultural dimension to the stories. I made some word cards and talked about the pictures, introducing words as I did so. Pilar soon knew the characters and said things like 'Floppy walking' and 'Look girl football', which surprised her. We did some work on assembling sentences and copying them down, using the 'Breakthrough to Literacy' approach. Pilar told me what was happening in one of the pictures and I worked up what she said into written English. She read the sentence back to me, then we cut it into individual words and she reassembled them.

Pilar: 'Look girl football'.

Teacher: 'Look, the girl is playing football'.

This is a good opportunity to teach a particular construction by repetition. 'Floppy is running', 'Biff is walking' and so on. It is also providing models of correct English rather than giving the more negative message of correcting mistakes.

A colleague of mine translated the story into Spanish and Pilar and I wrote our own bilingual version of the story together.

18th Jan: I checked Pilar's vocabulary using the cards from Tap Tap. She is now using everyday transactional phrases confidently, such as 'I get the pencil.', 'I don't understand', 'what's this?' She had learned *book, door, pencil, tree, present, banana, apple, flower(s), telephone, elephant,* but not *teddy bear, ball, house, dress, chair, bus, lorry, bird, glasses.* It is easy to see that the words she learnt first were generally those she encountered frequently in the classroom, where she was using English. Some of the less common words, such as *elephant* are the same, or very similar, in Spanish. As with first language acquisition nouns, which are tangible and often easy to illustrate through games such as Tap Tap, are learnt first.

She had made some progress with handwriting and there was positive feedback from home about the bilingual book. I asked her mother to obtain a small Spanish/English dictionary. I would show Pilar how to use it and she could then find words she wanted in both languages herself. I also helped her mother to make contact with the County library and checked with the librarian there about their range of Spanish books.

Having made good progress with settling in, we were ready to write a plan for her next stage. Using the Kent Language and Achievement Support Service assessment framework, I checked Pilar's language level and wrote some language targets for her. These I discussed with her class teacher. Using level descriptions like these enables teachers to assign an approximate overall language stage to pupils and to identify specific targets to teach towards.

Listening	Follows simple spoken instructions with visual clues
	Responds to everyday words or phrases
	Makes sense of gist of general class instructions
Speaking	May use one or two word utterances
	Has a basic everyday vocabulary; classroom equipment, school geography, parts of body, time, colours, greetings.
	Can pronounce all English sounds
Reading	Recognises all letters and high frequency words. Secure knowledge of Oxford Reading Tree Stage 2 vocabulary
Writing	Forms all English letters correctly. Proper word spacing. Uses capitals and lower case correctly. Continues to record in detail in Spanish where appropriate. Words and phrases in English.
Maths	Telling the time, English money

These simple targets enabled us to set language aims in Pilar's mainstream curriculum experience. It is usually possible to establish a set of language targets within any given lesson, but at this stage during my visits to the school I mixed in-class support, group withdrawal and individual withdrawal, depending on what the class was doing and what I felt Pilar's needs were.

29th Jan Today I observed while a couple of groups played 'Tap Tap'. They have taught the game to other children in the class and can now play independently. It seems to be helping Pilar to form friendships and to use a few short English phrases. I have often seen how pupil-pupil talk races ahead of the more formal language with adults in the classroom. Bilingual pupils seem to understand their classmates more easily in the playground than in the classroom!

I introduced *Guess Who*, another favourite of mine for developing social interaction at this early stage. *Guess Who* is manufactured by MB Games (Milton Bradley Ltd, Reevesland Industrial Estate, Main Avenue South, Newport, Gwent). The game consists of two sets of 24 faces mounted on plastic racks. The same faces also appear on a set of cards. Each player (two players) chooses a card. The idea of the game is to work out by elimination which character your opponent has. Players take it in turns to ask a question such as 'are you a man or a woman?' 'do you wear glasses?' 'have you got a hat?'. Each time the player gets an answer, he or she can eliminate a set of faces. The first to guess their opponent's character is the winner. The game builds vocabulary: facial characteristics, colours, sizes etc, and also enables work to be done on simple questions. As it is visual it is easy for the bilingual pupil to follow what is going on.

Pilar made good progress with this game, learnt the necessary vocabulary easily and tried whole sentences, for example:

'Is you pictures?' for 'Is this your picture?' and 'Is the man glasses? for 'Has the man got glasses?'

8th Feb Today we concentrated on the alphabet; letter names, sounds and shapes lower case and capitals, and alphabetical order. We also practised using the bilingual dictionary. I was pleased to see that Pilar had borrowed a bilingual story from the library.

15th Feb In class support, science. The class was writing up an experiment to see whether plants need leaves. After a talking stage, in which Pilar and I discussed the experiment using the actual objects used as cues, I differentiated the writing task to two stages;

What we used: soil, plants, scissors, sunlight, water. Vocabulary and simple subject verb object sentence structure.

What we did: I wrote four sentences giving the basic steps of the experiment on cards for sequencing, using straightforward sentence structures. The writing task was therefore converted to a more accessible reading task, followed by copying out, but using language appropriate to her stage of development in English.

> We put 2 plants in pots.
> We cut the leaves off 1 plant.
> We gave the plants some water.
> We left the plants in the room.

Unaided writing

In contrast to her fluency in writing Spanish, Pilar's free writing in English looks like early infant writing, although elements show developing knowledge of how English works (see opposite).

Pilar is having trouble with;

* contracted forms, it's

* t for d, s for th

* the letter I, sound i, confused with E

* friend, eating, balloon, wearing; all except balloons written roughly as spoken

Monday 1st March

is my birsday ant E(i) ant my fent E(a) etin crisps ant the it boll bos a – was weri a hat.

It's my birthday and I and my friend are eating crisps and there are balloons and I was wearing a hat.

Her writing from 15th March shows the difference in confidence and fluency between the English, which was largely copied and the Spanish which was free writing. At this stage she did not yet seem to relate the letters and their formation in Spanish to the similar requirements of an English writing task.

With writing tasks that were set for the whole class, I started by asking Pilar what she wanted to say and helped her to articulate her thoughts in English. I then asked her to write what she had told me, concentrating on the syntax, spelling of high frequency words and regular spelling patterns. Keeping the writing process firmly rooted in her own spoken words enabled the task to be meaningful and purposeful and ensured that she was not expected to produce writing that was ahead of her level of spoken competence. In some cases we finished with the word processor to achieve a polished product.

Monday. 15 March

one day jim Landed on
un dia un niño estaba en in Planeta
"le pregunta la nima dande biler
Le dise "¿tiene familia)" no dese el
niño pero por que estas a que Le
dise alaaler tu te raler las la,
estar un paco dan de biler no se
cano el chamar Jim i cano estar
no biene (¿por que se me muria
la familea por que mare de dan
de biler de un Planeta pueda gugar
si gugaro a can la pelota gugaza
i gugorian i ase can sonon "ero
se cororon la fueron a les
pedir se o adias adios adios

Other subject areas March 99: Many bilingual learners demonstrate strengths in Mathematics, because there are opportunities to become free of language hurdles but Pilar was beginning to struggle in Maths. I started to schedule in some in-class support during Maths lessons. Pilar showed that her knowledge of times tables was not fully secure yet (she's not alone here though in a Year 3 class!). Also, her counting beyond 20/30 was a little shaky (the names of the numbers are of course a language issue), so I gave her some practice in counting, clearly distinguishing '...ty' from '...teen'.

In History, the topic was the Romans. Pilar joined in class plenary sessions, where the material presented by the teacher was well supported with pictures. Her written work included a sequencing task supported by pictures.

> **Roman men at the baths**
> First they take their clothes off.
>
> Next they play with a ball and lift weights.
>
> They have a rest in warm water.
>
> They sweat in the hot room.
>
> A slave scrapes off the sweat with a strigil.
>
> They stand in cold water.
>
> They have a swim.

She also had the support of a textbook with pictures that could be labelled using simple sentences.

The Geography topic was 'the local area', which was in some ways useful for a newly-arrived pupil but also problematic where prior knowledge was assumed.

In Science, Pilar participated with enthusiasm in a class practical session in which the children described and classified rock samples. Simplified, scaffolded language such as 'Rocks are hard or soft. Rocks are rough or smooth. Rocks are one colour or many colours' enabled her to access the curriculum and build some language skills at word and sentence level. The practical task kept the language in context by providing good contextual cues to understanding. As her support teacher, I could show her hard and soft, rough and smooth etc. In follow-up work other subject-verb-adjective sentences could be rehearsed. This approach, similar to the type of syllabus used by English as a Foreign Language practitioners, was strengthened by building on aspects of the pupil's experiences in the mainstream setting. Withdrawal for intensive language instruction, sometimes seen as an alternative, would deny this opportunity and, in my opinion, hamper the learning process.

One word of caution: the passive voice often used to generalise in Science (and in other curriculum areas), can be difficult for bilingual pupils for two reasons. Firstly, word orders may break the active pattern and secondly, subject and object may be less obvious. So, for example, 'Chalk is made by the sea' fits the subject-verb-adjective pattern well ('Chalk is white') but it breaks the pattern illustrated by 'We made a model cliff'. However 'The sea makes chalk' is not really full or clear enough for Year 3, so I would opt for something like 'Bones from sea animals fall down to the sea bed. There they get squashed together very hard. After millions of years, they turn into chalk.' It is vital at this early stage to have a careful look at the language used in curriculum delivery and strike a purposeful balance between simplifying for meaning and developing the bilingual pupil's language.

> **March – May** Pilar's confidence continued to grow. I noticed that she was willing to try answering questions in front of the whole class, even when she misunderstood the question, which confirmed that the class atmosphere was supportive: nobody takes the risk that they may be ridiculed. She even took a turn in a class assembly and told the whole school 'what makes me happy' (when she sees her Dad). In a class plenary session on the weather she was able to tell the class about South American weather, especially Tierra del Fuego, which she had visited. Such contributions of specialised knowledge from first-hand experience are extremely valuable opportunities to build the bilingual pupil's self-esteem and to develop attitudes and perspectives in the class as a whole.

For the next few visits I concentrated on some basic Maths skills, because Pilar's Maths appeared weak, possibly because of differences in the two educational systems. Teaching young bilingual pupils Maths is very like teaching monolingual pupils: it is frequently a case of finding the mode of learning that works for the particular pupil: verbal, spatial, formulaic, practical. Pilar seemed to have missed out on any work on place value so I focused on this. There are some language issues here: for example some of the ways we express multiplication derive from vernacular language and need attention with bilingual pupils: *'times'*, *'five threes'*, *'lots of'*, *'groups of'* and so on. Similar considerations apply to fractions, which Pilar encountered in April. In both cases, multiplication and fractions, using supportive material helped to develop her conceptual grasp of the topic. Another problem area for her was subtraction using a number line. Again, her lack of experience of place value appeared to be holding her back, so we looked at patterns such as 33-23, 47-17, 78-58 etc. Work on rounding numbers and approximating answers also caused difficulty; here again the concept is wrapped up in language that we use widely outside Maths; e.g 'roughly, close to, nearest' etc. By demonstrating a mathematical process such as rounding to the nearest 10, I was able to help Pilar tackle the concept and to introduce the language through her understanding. It is possible that she might have encountered similar language in other areas but at this stage I suspect she understood it purely as a mathematical item.

Pilar's spoken English had by now advanced considerably and she was speaking in full sentences – with errors – and asking questions well. She also used common idioms and contractions such as 'what's that?' She still had difficulty pronouncing 'th' (pronounced 't') , hard 'g', 'b' and 'v', so 'gave' sounded like 'chab'. Some coaching helped her to say 'th' and 'g' but she couldn't manage 'b/v'. By leading her through 'f' (unvoiced) for 'v' (voiced), I hoped to enable her to pronounce the sound the English way. This approach helped, but has not yet fully cleared up the matter. 'Gafe' for 'gave' sounds better to the English listener and of course many English accents retain this pronunciation.

July: Unaided writing

It is interesting to track Pilar's development in completely unaided writing.

> Monday 1st March: 'is my birsday ant E(i) ant my fent E(a) etin crisps ant the it boll bos a – was weri a hat.'
>
> *It's my birthday and I and my friend are eating crisps and there are balloons and I was wearing a hat.*
>
> 7th July: 'yoy gen da to be pages' for *'you can go to the penguins'*. This was the slogan she wrote for a travel poster advertising Tierra del Fuego as a holiday destination.

In some ways, looking at this snippet, there seems to have been little progress in four months, but close analysis reveals development. Firstly, the sentence is grammatically correct, including the correct use of the potential auxiliary 'can'. 'Yoy' for 'you' probably arises because of the tricky names and sounds of y and u, and should improve as Pilar builds her sight vocabulary. The word 'you' is much more common in speech than in text. 'Gen' for 'can' and 'be' for 'the' shows pronunciation imprecision and 'da' for 'go' was probably written in desperation after using 'g' as a 'c' in 'gen' for 'can'. 'Penguin' is one of those words that you either know if you've learnt it or don't if you haven't! It is also one of those words that is likely to be more or less the same in many languages. If she had used the Spanish, 'pinguino', she would have been closer than her attempt in English, but bilingual pupils rarely substitute their first language for a word they don't know.

This account ends with a book that Pilar wrote in July, close to the end of term. This was an extended writing task and she had some help from various adults and classmates at different stages. I think it illustrates the point from the introduction: however carefully and systematically we plan our teaching and however thoroughly we monitor progress, learning is not a linear activity. As learners, we progress in fits and starts. We are inconsistent, we forget things, we do something right in one sentence and the same thing wrong in the next. We astound our teachers by succeeding in an impossibly difficult task and then confound them by failing an absurdly easy one. Teaching is as much craft as science and planning is necessary but it's not a universal panacea. Without it we might stumble and struggle, but with it we still weave in and out of the straight track through the forest!

I would love to attach a video clip of Pilar telling this story or better still, chatting to her friends about her likes and dislikes – that would really show you how far she has come in six months. But the written version of 'The parrot who could talk' will have to do. I want you to imagine it being read in an enchanting Spanish accent by a little girl with shiny black hair that falls into her big brown eyes. As I write this I almost regret that I'm trying to 'correct' her pronunciation and deny her perhaps a small piece of her individuality.

The parrot who coud tauk

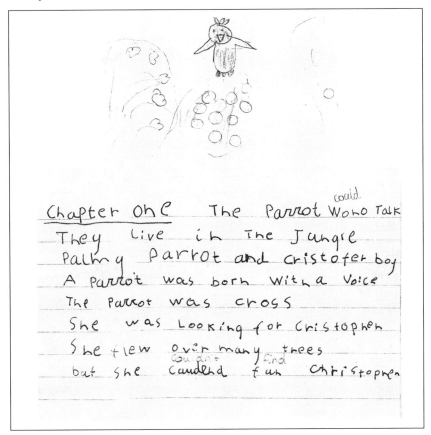

chapter one The parrot wold talk

They live in the jungle Palmy Parrot and Cristofer boy. A parrot was born with a voice. The parrot was cross She was looking for Christopher She few over many trees but she caudend fun Christopher.

chapter 2

Palmy goes to find Chiristophar bat she couldnt finid hem She gou tu the water to look but she culdnt fin him She starten to sign (*started to sing*) She fin Cristafer The gau to a park

chapter 3

Chistopher gau in I hause (*confusing 'a' meaning one, with number one*) Palmy gau to Pamy + tall Chistopher Pamy gau look oo I gau Alright yes les gau haum I dandt loic bin Pamy gau sllep Chistoper gau slepp.

Christopher went to Palmy's house and Palmy told Chritopher 'Palmy went to look (for him.) (Palmy said) 'Oh (can) I go?' 'Alright yes' 'Let's go home I don't like being (here). Palmy went to sleep. Christopher went to sleep.

4

Mufaro's Beautiful Daughters: Promoting first languages within the context of the Literacy Hour

Maggie Gravelle

The Literacy Hour, now firmly established in most schools in England can be seen as a scaffold or a straitjacket, depending on your viewpoint. Many teachers have used the Framework to continue the imaginative and supportive work they have been doing with classes which include bilingual learners. But if the National Literacy Strategy is inadequate, as I believe it is, in the guidance it offers for teaching bilingual learners, it has even less that is helpful for developing children's first language skills.

Section 4 of the Framework for Teaching (DfEE, 1998) has a part headed 'Children with English as an Additional Language (EAL)'. The extent to which EAL has become a formulaic label is indicated by the minimal reference to additional languages, those other than English, in the text. It is acknowledged that some children will 'be literate in languages other than English' but information about, and development of, these skills is seen mainly in the context of learning English. 'Their literacy skills' it is suggested, 'may be a significant factor in their success in learning English.' (DfEE, 1998:106) Later it is recognised that 'talking about literacy in languages other than English can help EAL pupils to identify points of similarity and difference between languages at word, sentence and text level' (DfEE, 1998:107). And it encourages discussion of reading and writing in home languages in order to build confidence in 'tackling tasks in English'. Key concepts can on occasion be introduced in the home language.

For teachers with little experience of, or confidence in, promoting home languages in the classroom there is little in the document to encourage further exploration. Yet we know that maintenance of first language significantly enhances pupils' personal identity. Links between home and school, between generations and across cultures are more positive and fruitful if bilingualism is actively encouraged. In addition much research suggests that cognitive and linguistic development are improved with the flexibility and sensitivity engendered by using more than one language. Cummins (1996), in his review of international research into the policies and practices of teaching bilingual students, presents compelling evidence that continued development of first languages supports the acquisition of a second and probably also contributes to cognitive development. The work of Virginia Collier and Wayne Thomas (see Ovando and Collier, 1998; Collier and Thomas, 1999) confirms the value of continued first language use and development in furthering academic success and subsequent language acquisition.

In more and more schools and classrooms there is evidence of sound multicultural practice. Resources which reflect a range of cultures are readily available and teachers are aware of the importance of using them to reinforce learning and to establish positive attitudes. But the Literacy Hour, while broadening the range of genres to which children are introduced has actually restricted the texts in use. Publishers have been quick to respond to the need for resources for the Literacy Hour, including big books, some of which limit rather than extend pupils' experiences. Traditional tales at Key Stage 1 for example, seldom go beyond Little Red Riding Hood and The Three Little Pigs.

Support for bilingual learners is often marginalised, fragmentary and confined to those with little English. Such support is almost always aimed at improving English skills, and recognition and encouragement of the development of first languages is rare. In classes fortunate enough to have bilingual support assistants their role is all too often to translate instructions and text so that children who cannot yet follow the lesson in English have greater access to the curriculum and the work of the class. Such support is generally withdrawn as soon as pupils can operate confidently in English.

Recently I worked in a Year 3/4 class with Seema, a bilingual teacher for whom first language maintenance was important, to evaluate ways of developing this within the Literacy Hour. Although few children in the class shared the same language and no-one spoke Seema's language, Hindi, we were clear about the value of using and building on their multilingual experiences. Most of the monolingual English speakers were bidialectal and several bilingual learners were fluent writers as well as speakers of more than one language. There were also several bilingual children at an early stage of English language acquisition.

Park School is a multi-ethnic, multilingual primary school in the inner city. Families in the area come from many parts of the world, including the far East, Africa and the Indian sub-continent. The school has made close links with the local community, partly through the well established Section 11, now Ethnic Minority Achievement Support team, who amongst other initiatives, have introduced a family literacy scheme. Information about religion, home languages, country of origin and parental literacy is routinely collected and used positively to offer support to children and parents. So Seema held considerable information about the skills and experiences of the children in her class, even though, as she acknowledged, working closely with a group afforded her additional insights.

Within the Literacy Hour we aimed to develop strategies and resources for both bilingual and monolingual children to extend their literacy in English but also to reinforce the value and importance of community languages.

We chose as a text *Mufaro's Beautiful Daughters* by John Steptoe, for several reasons. The tale is a version of Cinderella and would therefore be familiar to many of the children, and the central character is a strong black woman. It met the range specified the National Literacy Strategy for that term (Y3T2) in being a traditional story and having a theme relating to other tales. It is well written, with attractive illustrations which we knew would appeal to the children. We considered this important and agreed that we would resist using any text that was badly written, uninteresting or had no relevance to the pupils. *Mufaro's Beautiful Daughters* is a challenging text for some Year 3 children and therefore more suitable for shared than independent reading. We anticipated that the story, set in Africa, might enable the black and bilingual children to bring their knowledge of a range of cultures and practices to the text and to the class. However, one cannot assume that all children will have, or be willing to share, detailed knowledge of cultures which we assume to be theirs. Opportunities for children to be the experts must be created without exerting pressure. Seema's knowledge of her class, their previous learning and their likely responses, reinforced the decision to select this book.

We realised that some of the children would find listening to the story demanding. Some would have difficulty in following the text and for others the unfamiliar setting might be a barrier. There were also some linguistic aspects of the story that could present difficulties, particularly to the bilingual learners. However, we also knew that the children were becoming accustomed to the organisation of the Literacy Hour and that an ethos had been developed of interest in and acceptance of linguistic diversity.

The session began with shared reading of *Mufaro's Beautiful Daughters: An African Tale*. Seema introduced the story to the class and discussed the pictures and the setting. Children immediately began discussing the front cover. One child said, 'She's beautiful' and another commented, 'She looks evil.' They noticed from the illustration and the subtitle that the setting was Africa and went on to talk about the difference between a tale and a story. Some children already knew the story and Seema gave them a listening focus by asking them to look out for anything they had forgotten. For others the tale was new and they were already anticipating some of the events.

During the reading children were attentive and made remarks like, 'They wear their hair like that (in Africa)' or 'She won't be queen'. Even though the reading took some time few children lost attention and many were enthralled. We agreed that this first reading had to give all pupils a feel for the plot and the characters. Even the emergent bilingual learners were carried along by the story and supported by the pictures and by hearing and seeing the text simultaneously. Seema seldom interrupted her reading to clarify a point. I have observed situations when the teacher keeps stopping to ask questions, make grammatical points or comment on phonics. This breaks the flow and can prevent bilingual learners in particular from engaging with the full story. On the other hand in any shared reading session the pace is inevitably set by the teacher, who must be sensitive to the need some pupils may have to stop and interrogate the text at various points.

A group of children then worked with the teacher on the text. They immediately began to discuss the story and pictures and to relate them to their own experiences. It was clear that they had all understood the gist and each noticed different details. Emmanuel (Nigerian background, monolingual English) was particularly taken by the picture of the boy with 'fairy' ears and Viet (Vietnamese background, speaks English, Cantonese and Vietnamese) was interested in the differences between the two sisters, one of whom he described as 'feisty'. Queenet (Nigerian background, monolingual English) made the link with another story set in Africa.

Two children, both Cantonese speakers, started discussing wedding customs and switched automatically into their first language when they couldn't think of the English phrase. This generated a comparison to weddings in Nigeria and Vietnam. Queenet and Emmanuel said, 'In Nigeria we wear clothes like this', pointing to one of the illustrations. Until now Anna, the only Portuguese speaker and a relatively new arrival to the school, had said nothing although she had listened attentively. She burst into the conversation to describe Portuguese wedding customs and the party and 'holiday' that followed it. These discussions provided a valuable opportunity for the children, and especially the bilingual learners, to revisit the text and bring their own experiences to that exploration. It also gave the listening teachers insights into the children's interests, abilities and experiences that are too easily buried in the business of a classroom.

There was an additional, unexpected contribution when Anna, the Portuguese girl, did not know the word for antler and looked it up in the dictionary that she always carried with her. She remarked that there were two words in Portuguese for the same English term and went on the speculate about why this was so and how the words differed. She also explained that Portuguese uses different vowel sounds from English. Even with her limited skills in English she could articulate some of her metalinguistic knowledge.

There was a real purpose for re-telling the story the following day when Michelle (Vietnamese background, speaks Cantonese and English), who had been absent, rejoined the group. We had planned to begin some written retelling of the story with the support of a writing frame, but it was clearly important that Michelle was given the opportunity to understand the book fully. I had brought in a yam, a vegetable mentioned in the story, and this generated discussion in English and first language about how it was grown and cooked. As with the discussion of wedding customs, giving children the confidence to bring their own cultural experiences into the classroom makes them more comfortable about using their home language. We also felt that although the talk delayed the planned writing activity, it enabled all the children to approach their writing with more confidence. The teacher meanwhile scribed some of the relevant words and phrases onto a flip chart.

For the third session we wanted children to start writing their own versions of the tale. We began by re-reading the text, stressing the cohesive structure. We wanted to help learners articulate some of their implicit knowledge about narrative structure and relate this to other stories they knew. Children discussed the beginning, 'A long time ago...' which identifies the genre, and made alternative suggestions which were written on the flip chart. We then discussed the linguistic features that moved the story onwards, such as 'after travelling...', ' it was not yet dawn when...' and so on. They were able to identify these confidently in talk with peer support. The phrases were recorded on the chart to be remembered and reused when it came to writing. It often helps bilingual learners when spoken language is reinforced in written form.

The children were then given a writing frame to support their writing of their version of the story. Again, we encouraged discussion, particularly about the main characters and their personalities. Anna did not know the term 'unkind' and one of the other pupils explained that it was the opposite of kind. This led to a spontaneous, brief conversation about other 'un-' words. The names of the characters, Mufaro, Manyara and Nyasha, were also a matter of interest and Emmanuel (Nigerian), explained that some names have meaning and he illustrated this with his own name. The value of sharing through talk was continually reinforced. Complex and unusual vocabulary was discussed and it was noticeable that this vocabulary was reused by several of the children in both their subsequent writing and their talk. Trung (Vietnamese background, speaks Vietnamese and English) says very little in class. In the context of the group he displayed sensitive understanding and wide vocabulary, although he was still reluctant to use his Vietnamese. He remembered 'teased' and 'chores' from the story and used them in context. Later he added that the tale was set, 'in a village in Africa – an African village.' The bilingual children understood, perhaps more readily than some of their classmates, the ways a village differs from a town. Seema noticed that their contributions were much longer than is usual in a whole class situation. This was partly because of the time and space that they had to listen and be listened to. The small group context undoubtedly gave them confidence to make mistakes without fear of ridicule or correction.

They were also able to check understanding with each other as well as the teacher. Viet was re-reading part of the text 'Manyara, a servant in the queen's household' and asked, 'What's that... household?' Seema's response: 'The queen's family... quarters... where they live... all servants together' gave alternative meanings and led to a discussion about servants' jobs, including cleaning the house and hoovering the floor.

On transcribing some of this discussion it was apparent that the bilingual learners possessed understanding and skills that can sometimes be missed. Viet, who in class rarely does more than answer direct, closed questions said, '*The other way she was going through the path she saw an old woman. She said, ' you see a lot of trees that will laugh at you and you mustn't be scared and you mustn't laugh back and you see a man has his head tucked under his arm and must be kind to him.' she said to the old woman... ugly old lady. Then on the path she saw trees laughing at her and she said 'I'll laugh back at you' She just ran past old man without speaking to her.'* Viet retold this part of the story, which clearly caught his imagination, at great speed and with animation. His fluency in English, frequently disguised in class, is evident. He can use a range of tenses, use most pronouns correctly and construct negatives.

Finding time for extended writing is a matter of concern within the Literacy Framework. We decided to devote a whole session to writing so that the children could complete and share a piece of work. They were all now familiar with the story and had completed outline planning frames. We had also ensured that some of the key words and phrases were written on the flip chart for reference and reminded the pupils about aspects of cohesion discussed earlier. Despite encouraging paired writing, each child in fact wanted to complete their own story. Viet found this activity very demanding, although the planning stage helped him. He finally produced a story which was the longest he had written and which drew on the aspect of the text he had talked about most. Although he would not read his story to the whole class he had the confidence to read it to the small group.

The slookt wood

One day Two little girl one of the them was bin sloot by a old man he sich his heed off his nek and ladid on the girl and she seem Hlep and The ufvr sister ckan and wen she was raning she flhe in the rivver and gawd in wood rivver but uf sister fatd.

(The Spooked Wood
One day two little girls, one of them was being spooked by an old man. He swished his head off his neck and landed on the girl and she screamed, 'Help!' and the other sister came and when she was running she fell in the river and goed in wood river, but the other sister fainted.)

Anna, who had also done some writing in Portuguese, showed considerable ability in her narrative structure, pace and use of direct speech. She used her dictionary competently and consequently made relatively few spelling errors, although her use of past tense, for example, is still not secure. She was also very independent, having her Portuguese literacy experience and skill to support her writing in English.

Dual text books are found in many classrooms and it is interesting to monitor their use. I have found that except in schools where there are relatively large numbers of bilingual learners and where their languages are given importance, the dual text books are often relegated to a small, unobtrusive area of the book corner and rarely used, even by bilingual pupils. If such books are to have a place in raising the status of community languages they need to form a part of all children's reading experiences and be valued and shared by the teacher.

For our final sessions on *Mufaro's Beautiful Daughters* we wanted the children in our group to work on a bilingual version of their stories. Though they were not all literate in their first languages we anticipated that their families or friends might be able to help them and also suggested taped oral retellings in community languages which could then be transcribed. Seema began the session by telling a version of Cinderella, which has many similarities to *Mufaro's Beautiful Daughters*, in Hindi. Although none of the class spoke Hindi we were all able to pick out some familiar words and to appreciate the tone and music of the language. It was an un-rehearsed recounting which reassured pupils that not every teller has to be fully fluent and polished on every occasion. It also signalled that other languages have a place in an English medium classroom and that literature is not exclusively English.

Pupils in groups then looked at a selection of dual language texts. We encouraged them to speculate about the languages and even to try to 'read' those that used a Roman alphabet. Queenet and Emmanuel were looking at a Yoruba book and laughing about some of their own attempts to pronounce the words. They agreed that although they did not speak Yoruba they had both heard members of their families use a Nigerian language. This was the first intimation for anyone in the school that these pupils had access to languages other than English. They began to notice the recurrence of certain words in the Yoruba story and speculated about how these related to the English version.

We discussed the idea that they could try decoding Yoruba, whereas a script such as Punjabi would be totally inaccessible. This led to an investigation of features the children could recognise in other scripts, such as punctuation and directionality. Certain combinations of letters or symbols were noticed. Children who could recognise and read different forms of writing gained status and this led to discussion about how and where they had learnt. Viet, Michelle and Trung all talked about the community language schools they attended on Saturdays.

For the final writing task we tried to put literate bilinguals together with monolingual peers to work together on a dual language text. Success varied according to the literacy skills of the bilingual partners. In one threesome Anna was able to write a Portuguese story with little assistance from the two monolingual English speakers, whose roles were therefore diminished. In another group, where skills were better matched, co-operation was evident and the story developed quickly. Understanding what pupils bring to a task needs to be refined in order to inform effective planning.

Inevitably some aspects of the sessions were more successful than others. The ethos of the class, established by Seema, was one of support for and interest in languages. This was helped by Seema's own bilingualism, but every teacher can learn, often from the children, a few phrases and greetings in languages other than English. More importantly, we can all show an interest in other dialects and languages and encourage investigation and discussion. We were surprised at how much we learnt about the children's linguistic skills. Once this becomes a valid and valued area to share, even an apparently monolingual class will usually reveal families with multi-lingual and multidialectal backgrounds or histories. Children who speak only English will often contribute the few words of Spanish they may have picked up on holiday, or, more importantly, begin to reflect on and value their dialectal fluency and ability to code-switch.

Time for the pupils, and particularly the bilinguals, to talk was vital to their increased success and confidence. This has implications for organisation and class management within the constraints of the Literacy Hour. We unashamedly deviated from the structure on occasion, although the overall balance and framework remained. We agreed that opportunities for all children to recall, recap and rehearse was important and aimed for quality processes rather than quantity in terms of product. At other times we might plan for breadth rather than depth of coverage, but one needs to be clear about the balance between the two and the trade-off of one against the other. Independent activities do not have to be individual activities. Children in Seema's class were accustomed to working together and sharing, but this does not happen automatically and needs to be carefully planned. The benefits for all learners and especially bilinguals, are enormous.

We aimed to use shared and guided writing sessions, supported by talk, to move the children towards independence and modelling was often the first and most important step. We tried to be precise in our planning and explicit in our teaching about expectations for the writing. Frames were used as supports, coming at an intervening stage between talk and continuous writing. The frames were more helpful for some children than others. In several cases they merely resulted in duplication with little amendment or development, when the children simply copied their writing from the frames to their stories. There was a danger that they were used in a ritualised way and we were aware that, like many teachers, we were probably asking for too much writing. However several pupils wrote more extensively and with a greater sense of achievement than ever before. They also had the satisfaction of achieving a permanent, personal record of their ideas.

We were particularly pleased when children had the confidence to reject the frames. Stories are not always planned from character and setting to conflict and resolution, the way so many writing frames suggest. Ability to use and then discard the scaffolding is important for pupils and must become part of a teacher's monitoring and planning.

The bilingual learners valued the reassurance of small group work. They felt more secure in taking risks and asking for guidance than in whole class situations. The composition of the group was carefully planned and based on Seema's knowledge of the social, linguistic and cognitive skills of her class. Teachers gradually acquire this understanding but should remain flexible and plan the groups according to the support children need and can obtain from each other, rather than to a fixed idea of ability. Different abilities are revealed in different contexts and we learnt as much from and about the children as they did.

The planning gave prominence to language and to explicit teaching and discussion about language. The Literacy Strategy places great emphasis on this aspect of learning and teachers are generally gaining confidence in their teaching of language. The children's own metalinguistic abilities surprised and delighted us. Bilingual pupils often have both a great need for and a great understanding of linguistic feedback and we were clear that this had to be firmly contextualised. Frequent opportunities arose for explanations and discussions about the ways in which language clarifies meaning. We didn't need to invent or contrive them, merely to grasp and develop them. And we achieved this because we were working closely with one group of children but also because our planning anticipated and prepared for many of the eventualities.

The National Literacy Strategy has been introduced with the stated aim of raising basic skills in literacy. It has offered teachers a framework within which to achieve this and, through training and guidance materials, has enhanced their understanding of the structure of English. But, certainly in some classes, it has limited opportunities for children to use talk, collaboration and first language to promote enjoyment and engagement with text. Some teachers, intent on detailed planning for specific objectives, have lost confidence in their ability to respond to children's contributions, ideas and experiences and to build on these in ways which develop their understanding.

In virtually every classroom there is a range of dialects and languages, either among the pupils and their families or within the written and audio-visual resources, that can stimulate the development of linguistic and metalinguistic understanding. We remain convinced that it is both possible and desirable to respect and use first languages within the context of the Literacy Hour.

Resources
Steptoe, J (1987) *Mufaro's Beautiful Daughters*, Puffin Books

My thanks to Seema Agarwal and her pupils for their support, collaboration and guidance.

5
Bilingual Learners and Numeracy
Zaitun Virani-Roper

The National Numeracy Strategy has a special section on children learning English as an additional language (EAL). In it the good practice in teaching and learning that EAL specialists have been recommending for decades is emphatically restated. This chapter elaborates on these recommendations, while also exploring some of the barriers to implementation and inclusion.

EAL Pupils and the National Numeracy Strategy

This section of the introduction to the framework begins with a bold statement:

> Take care not to underestimate what children can do mathematically simply because they are new learners of the English language. (1)

It goes on the suggest that whole class sessions:

> can provide helpful adult models of spoken English, and opportunities for careful listening, oral exchange and supportive, shared repetition. (2)

and in group work that teachers will probably need to:

- repeat instructions for EAL pupils

- speak more clearly, emphasising key words, particularly when you are describing tasks that they are to do independently

- put picture cues on worksheets or puzzle cards

- simplify the words used, but not the mathematics (except where an EAL pupil also has special educational needs that warrant this). (3)

The document goes on to emphasise the importance of talk, peer-support and home-language support from pupils and adults.

In the plenary for example, teachers should:

- allow EAL pupils time to watch and listen to those fluent in English explaining and demonstrating their methods to the class using a board or flip chart

- invite them too to demonstrate, on the board or with apparatus

- avoid any pressure to accompany their demonstration with an oral explanation in English before they are ready. (4)

Here is a sound understanding of the importance of the 'silent period', which is sometimes wrongly interpreted to mean that bilingual children do not participate.

If taken on board by mainstream teachers these recommendations from the DfEE would allow bilingual pupils to make the progress of which they are capable and at the same time discourage the not uncommon practice of withdrawing pupils at the initial stages of English language development or grouping them with native English speakers who are experiencing learning difficulties.

In addition, the *National Numeracy Strategy* promotes inclusion by asking teachers to encourage bilingual pupils to:

join in things that all children do in chorus: counting, reading aloud whole number sentences, chanting, finger games, songs about numbers, and so on. The structure of rhymes, and the natural rhythm in songs and poems, play an important part in developing number sense in any culture. Try to use stories and rhymes that will support access to meaning for pupils from a range of cultural backgrounds. As soon as English language beginners are reasonably confident at saying something together with others, ask them to say it again on their own. Give them plenty of time and much praise for doing so, and also check for understanding. (5)

The section ends with a wonderful suggestion:

Get them to show the class the ways that numbers are spoken and written in their home language, and to demonstrate any board games or playground games that they know and which involve numbers. Children who speak and read only English are often fascinated by the similarities with the number system that they are familiar with and they too gain from the experience. (6)

In sum, the *National Numeracy Strategy* gives a clear message about the social, linguistic and cognitive inclusion of all pupils, including pupils at the initial stages of learning English, within the numeracy lesson.

The *Strategy* also emphasises the role of parents and classroom assistants in promoting high standards in numeracy. It argues that better standards of numeracy occur when:

- Classroom assistants take part in planning and are used effectively to support teachers in Mathematics lessons.

- Parents are kept well-informed and encouraged to be involved through discussions at school and sometimes in work with pupils at home. (7)

Unfortunately the commendable statements of intent have not been implemented in the actual training materials and few of the video training programmes demonstrate these principles in classroom practice. There are no specific case studies which train teachers in meeting the additional needs of bilingual pupils at the early stages of learning English. Similarly there are no strategies offered to schools on how they might involve parents who do not share the language, culture and context of the school.

Recently leaflets and videos have been translated for non-English speaking parents by the Basic Skills Agency. But they are translations of videos and leaflets prepared for English-speaking communities, which help only in so far as the non-English-speaking minorities can begin to understand what happens in English-speaking classrooms but do not enable them to engage their children meaningfully in Maths activities at home. This is largely because they are not grounded in the numeracy experiences of the home culture. Similarly these translations do not give teachers any confidence in involving bilingual parents in the life of the school because mere translations miss an important point. They do not emphasise the importance of the home language and home context in raising achievement.

I carried out the attached test (Figure 1) with staff who were specifically interested in bilingual issues and attended training delivered by the Ethnic Minority Achievement Service in Harrow, on numeracy or other EAL issues. Some were specialists funded by the Ethnic Minority and Traveller Achievement Grant, others were classroom assistants and a few were mainstream teachers with specialist responsibility for co-ordinating learning support at school level. All twenty-one responded either 'no' or 'don't know' to the statement: 'The National Numeracy Strategy gives guidance for EAL pupils in the numeracy lesson', suggesting that if colleagues who were specifically interested in EAL issues and attended voluntary

**"Test" your knowledge about:
EAL pupils in the National Numeracy Strategy**

- I have received training on the National Numeracy Strategy

    Yes / No

- The National Numeracy Strategy gives guidance on EAL pupils in the Numeracy lesson

    Yes / No, I don't know

- The training materials provide good examples of supporting EAL pupils in the classroom

    Yes / No, I don't know

- There is good advice on how to enable non English speaking parents to support their children

    True / False, I don't know

- There are some good ideas on setting home work that depicts home languages and the home contexts of refugee pupils

    True / False, I don't know

- My comments on the training I have received are:

Figure 1

training in their own time did not know whether the National Numeracy Strategy was offering guidance on inclusion of EAL pupils then it was highly unlikely that their colleagues at school level would know either.

Colleagues responded to the point: 'My comments on the training I have received are...' as follows:

- some very interesting activities, but many still need adapting for EAL pupils

- EAL pupils' needs are not addressed

- designed for middle class children in middle class schools

- very little about EAL pupils

- it is inadequate and has gaps.

This chapter tries to redress the balance by discussing three case studies which show the complexity of assessing bilingual pupils' mathematical knowledge, understanding and skills and demonstrate how the provision of well thought-out multilingual resources, including visual support, glossaries and bilingual dictionaries, can help access the Mathematics curriculum to these pupils. It also argues for the centrality of the role of bilingual and multilingual classroom assistants in not only supporting pupils and teachers but also encouraging parents and carers to be involved in the education of their children.

I often begin a training session by setting the task of counting the number of the letter 'f's in the following passage and then comparing results with a colleague.

How many 'f's?

Finished files are the result of years of scientific study combined with the experience of many years of experts.

With permission from Pacific Institute from their training pack on 'Investment in Excellence'.

Every time I have used this activity I have had colleagues reaching different totals. My hypothesis is that this is not because we cannot count, nor is it because we cannot read the letter 'f' but because it is a completely decontextualised exercise. We all have our own context with which we are familiar and feel comfortable and we all define the task differently. Mathematicians are keen to give children real life examples and contextualise maths problems within these life experiences but if our context is not their context and our language is not their language then instead of helping, the language and the context can obscure the mathematics.

CASE STUDY 1:

African child, home language Luganda, Age 10+, Spoken and written English age appropriate

I want to begin by relating an experience which has remained in my memory for many years since I left Uganda. I had an African child speaking Luganda in my class of ten year olds. We will call him Joshua. Once I set a question in an examination on fractions from a textbook. It read:

'I ate half an apple and half of what was left. What was left?'

As his answer, Joshua had written 'seeds'. I thought he had understood fractions since earlier in the term had worked out questions like $1/2 - 1/4$ or $1/2$ of $1/2$ correctly. In a later conversation with him, I asked, 'What would happen if I had an orange instead?' I was expecting an answer seeds/pips and peel. Instead of answering my question he asked, 'But what is an apple Miss?'. To the writers of that Maths textbook the fact that apples do not grow in Uganda was not significant. To Joshua, who was preoccupied with the meaning of apple rather than concentrating on the Maths content, it was a different story. Furthermore, how he knew that an apple had 'seeds' was another mystery to me, so I asked, 'How do you know that there are seeds in an apple?' 'I guessed it Miss,' was Joshua's honest reply.

CASE STUDY 2:

Japanese child, literate in Japanese, New arrival in Year 7 in middle school in Harrow – call her Yoko

I was teaching Yoko a few years ago at a school in Harrow. Her class teacher who was leading the Maths lesson had informed me that Yoko was literate in Japanese and well motivated. The teacher 'sensed' that she was a very able pupil. The class teacher had written the following on the board; 'What is the product of 12 and 11?' Yoko had read the question but did not understand the word 'product'. I therefore re-wrote the question using the mathematical symbol x as follows: 12 x 11=? Yoko did not read 'x' as a symbol for multiply, although she knew how to multiply and had seen the sign 'x' before. In this stressful situation she misunderstood 'x' as the symbol for an incorrect answer. She read it as a cross – a wrong answer.

She and I were both becoming frustrated when she took her dictionary out, looked up the word 'product', understood exactly what it meant, smiled and wrote 12 x 11 = 132.

With the *Numeracy Strategy* there is a booklet on *Mathematical Vocabulary*, but I wonder whether it is for pupil use or simply a teacher's tool. If it is the former then not only bilingual pupils but also many native English speakers would require a glossary with visual support where appropriate. Bilingual pupils would require glossaries, visual support and translations where relevant. Looking up one word – 'product' – had made Yoko's day! And mine. Long live the dual language dictionaries. In some LEAs including Harrow many glossaries have now been developed which are translated into the languages of the newly arriving pupil communities and are illustrated when appropriate.

CASE STUDY 3:

Afghan child, Farsi speaking, Year 3, born of an Afghan refugee mother. Mother literate in Farsi. The child had difficulties with left to right orientation

I was assessing Masud (not his real name) on place value using 3 digit numbers. Under **HTU** I wrote 234 and asked, 'Which number has the biggest value?'

Masud said, '4'.

This is a 'correct' answer because 4 is more than 3 or 2. I realised I had chosen a bad example, so I tried an alternative 2 digit number and an alternative strategy. I wrote 34 and asked, 'What's this number? Read it please.'

Masud: Thirty four

Me:	So the digit 3, is it 3 or 30?
Masud:	30.
Me:	Now let's go back to 234 (pointing to it). (I was careful not to say two hundred and thirty four.) Which has the bigger value, 3 or 4?
Masud:	(Pointing to 4) This is little bit little. (Pointing to 3) This is little bit big. (Pointing to 2) This big.

Now convinced that Masud did have a clear understanding of place value in 3 digit numbers, I set him the following addition:

$$HTU$$
$$234$$
$$+782$$

Masud added from left to right and gave the answer 917. For some time now I had been working on teaching Masud that questions like 23 take away 7 are written left to right, as

$$23-7=16.$$

Me:	Masud, look you've added from left to right, you need to start from right .... from units.
Masud:	Miss, remember left to right.

Off he went to play. We were both saved by the bell.

What this case study illustrates is how complex issues to do with mathematical conventions are, even without added complexities arising out of different cultural conventions.

Subsequently I spoke with our Farsi speaking classroom assistant who showed me how a division such as follows would be set out in Farsi.

$$10 \div 5 = 2 \text{ would be written as } \frac{10 \mid 5}{2}$$

instead of our convention

$$5 \mid \overline{\frac{2}{10}}$$

As an exercise in empathy I asked my colleagues to copy five divisions using the Farsi convention and imagine that they were copying their homework and that the lesson would end any minute. I will leave the result of this exercise to your imagination

Let me now turn to the third and the last aspect of this chapter which is to argue for importance of the role of bilingual and multilingual classroom assistants.

In Harrow we have established positive ways of working with bilingual classroom assistants. We carry out joint assessments of bilingual pupils using their home languages whenever possible. What we might previously have identified as a learning difficulty, we are now, with the help of bilingual learning assistants, often finding to be concept gaps due to missed schooling. As assessors we are fast learning not to equate concept gaps with learning difficulties. Furthermore we are finding that when targeted and well planned support is given to these late arrivals who have missed vital years of schooling and consequently developed concept gaps, they learn at an accelerated pace and can catch up remarkably quickly.

Our bilingual classroom assistants are also an invaluable asset in working alongside educational psychologists, educational social workers and other professionals.

If we as educators are serious about implementing the sound principles laid down in the *National Numeracy Strategy* then we need to set homework that reflects the children's home languages and cultures, especially if their parents are not fluent in English. We need to apply the bold statement made in the Strategy: 'Take care not to underestimate what children can do mathematically simply because they are new learners of the English language' to parents too. Just because parents do not speak English does not mean that they cannot support their children's learning. A clear message needs to be sent home that all languages are equally valid tools of teaching mathematics. Here the bilingual learning assistants are invaluable.

If we involve bilingual learning assistants in planning and deploy them effectively as the *Strategy* recommends then we can use them in the classroom to translate and access the curriculum at the time of direct teaching or group work or plenary. We can set aside time for them to translate tasks so we can provide 'different resources to

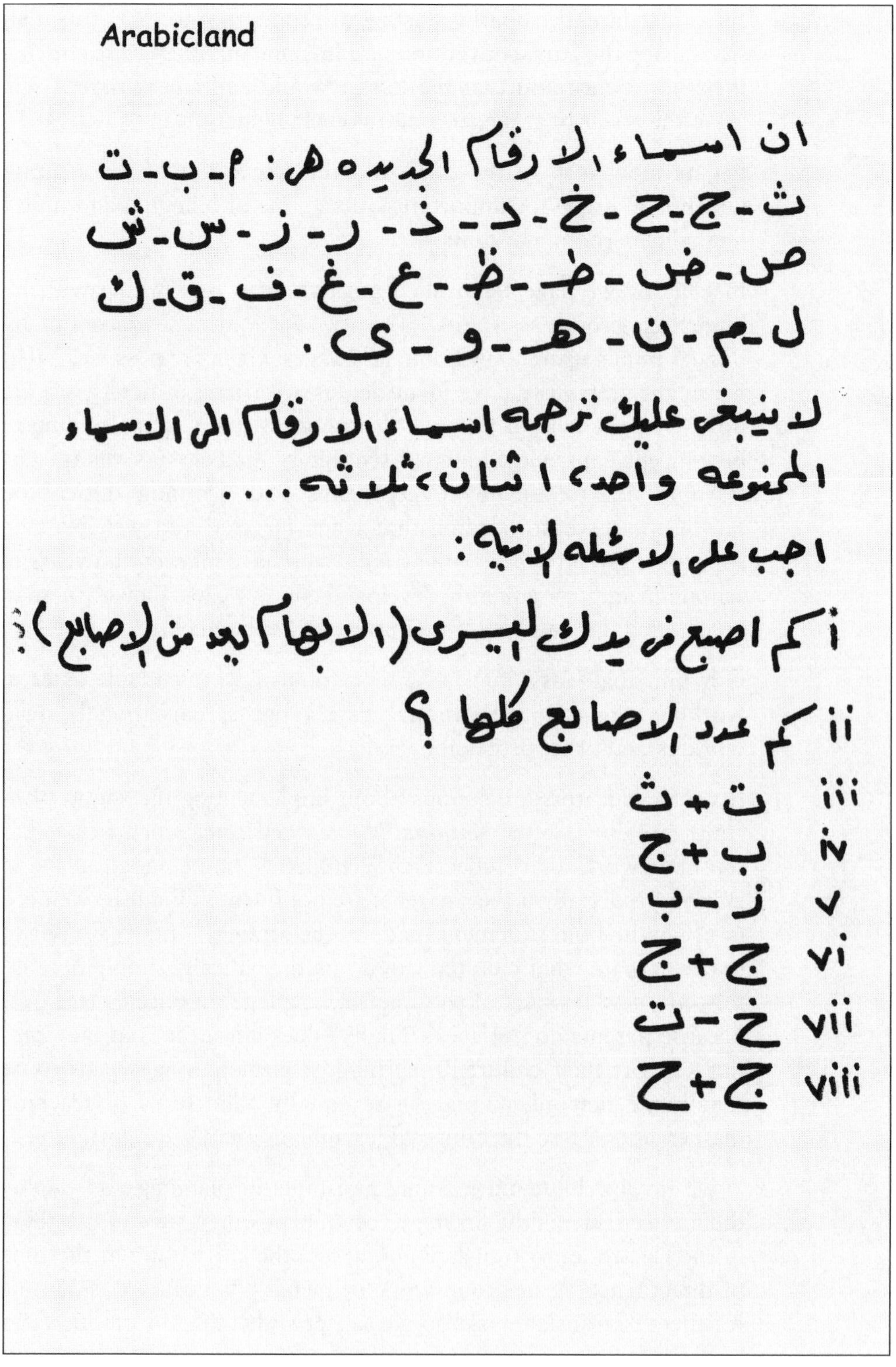

Arabicland

ان اسماء الارقام الجديده هي : م ـ ب ـ ت
ث ـ ج ـ ح ـ خ ـ د ـ ذ ـ ر ـ ز ـ س ـ ش
ص ـ ض ـ ط ـ ظ ـ ع ـ غ ـ ف ـ ق ـ ك
ل ـ م ـ ن ـ هـ ـ و ـ ى .

لا ينبغي عليك ترجمه اسماء الارقام الى الاسماء
الممنوعه واحد، اثنان، ثلاثه .....
اجب على الاسئله الاتيه :

أ كم اصبع في يدك اليسرى (لا بها م يعد من الاصابع)؟

ii كم عدد الاصابع كلها ؟

iii ت + ث

iv ب + ج

v ز ـ ب

vi ج + ج

vii خ ـ ت

viii ج + ح

Figure 2

Arabicland

The new number names are:
(Since the Service had no Arabic font at the time, the alphabet was hand written together with guidance as to directionality)
You must not translate these number names into the banned number names one, two, three, ...

Answer the following questions:

i　　How many fingers on your left hand (thumbs count as fingers)?

ii　　How many fingers do you have altogether?

iii　　ت + ث

iv　　ب + ج

v　　ز − ب

vi　　ح + ح

vii　　خ − ث

viii　　ج + ح

Extension questions, if you have time:

ix　　ث × ت

x　　ث ب

From an idea by Dr Ian Thompson, School of Education, University of Newcastle
Adapted for the whole class by Hassan Mostafa, Ethnic Minority Achievement Service, Harrow

Figure 3

support children working on the same task' (8). Figure 2 is an example of a task in Arabic that teachers can use in the numeracy lesson. In fact, the whole class could attempt the task on 'Arabicland' (Figure 3) as it serves the same objective as 'Alphabetland' (Figure 4). Additionally it would give a positive message to bilingual children while at the same time giving the English monolingual pupils an experience of functioning in the Arabic alphabet.

We need to be proactive in sending home materials that parents and children can talk about. Multilingual and multicultural resources can be sent home as well as used in the numeracy lesson. They show pupils and parents that we value their languages and use them in accessing the curriculum.

Recommending such strategies often elicits a response from schools such as: 'But children do not want to use their languages' or 'Parents do not like us to encourage home language support. They want their children to learn English as soon as possible'. These are genuine concerns and need to be addressed professionally. My reply is that we need to examine why any community might want to disown their language. What messages are we as educators giving to these communities? We say that we value other languages and cultures but often we do not go beyond 'Welcome' signs in different languages. Are we inadvertently giving a message that community languages are good enough for gestures but not for real learning? Sometimes we do not 'walk our talk'. 'Welcome' signs certainly contribute to an ethos of social inclusion. But if we are really serious about responsible inclusion we need to use the children's languages to access the curriculum and promote learning.

Are we taking the time and energy to explain to bilingual parents that if they want their children to learn Maths while they learn English then they need to work with us in supporting their children in their own language at home? Are we making it clear to parents that if we do not work together their children may develop concept gaps because their learning could be arrested while their English is being developed? Are we sharing with them the findings of all the research about how bilingual pupils learn? These are matters that we need to discuss with parents. And we can quote the guidance in the *National Numeracy Strategy* as our basis which will give tremendous credence to our argument. Bilingual learning assistants can

Alphabetland

The new number names are: A, B, C, D, ...

You must not 'translate' these number names into the banned number names one, two, three, ...

Answer the following questions:

   i How many fingers on your left hand (thumbs count as fingers)?

  ii How many fingers do you have altogether?

 iii C + D

  iv B + E

   v K − B

  vi E + E

 vii G − D

viii E + F

Extension questions, if you have time:

  ix D × C

   x D^B

From an idea by Dr Ian Thompson, School of Education, University of Newcastle

25 *The National* **Numeracy** *Strategy*

Figure 4

77

help us to talk with parents using their home languages and showing how learning can take place just as effectively in Albanian, Somali or Tamil.

Social inclusion can only be sustained if we work towards linguistic and cognitive inclusion. When refugees arrive in schools speaking no English they may be well motivated despite their trauma. They have a strong desire to communicate and succeed. We need to build on this high level of motivation and plan for responsible inclusion. If we do not, they soon become frustrated and may manifest their unmet learning need in unacceptable behaviour. Responsible inclusion is about recognising diversity and then acknowledging it. One way of acknowledging diversity is for schools to deploy specialist staff according to schools' needs and priorities. Bilingual staff who reflect the schools' diversity will go a long way to showing parents and pupils whose languages, cultures and life experiences are different from ours that educators are implementing, within the given constraints, our commitment to equality of opportunity. And such inclusion and recognition will be significant in fostering children's learning.

Notes

1 -5   DfEE (March 1999) *The National Numeracy Strategy: Framework for teaching mathematics from Reception to Year 6*, Crown copyright, London, page 22

6   Ibid; page 23

7   Ibid; page 5

8   DfEE (1999) *Three day course, Strategies for keeping the class together*, OHT 4.5, Crown copyright, London, page 20

6
Planning for Bilingual Learners Year 9 Geography: The EU and Italy
Steve Cooke and Susan Pike

When bilingual students achieve a fluency in spoken English which appears consistent with their native English speaking peers it is sometimes assumed that they no longer have language needs. This milestone is reached for many bilingual students in primary school and by secondary school they may be perceived as students who have learnt English and now need nothing in addition to the approaches, methods and classroom organisation the school provides for all students. Many educators, however, have suggested that even bilingual students who have received all their experience of formal education in the UK need a secondary curriculum which explicitly seeks to widen their linguistic repertoire and enhance their literacy skills.

Paradoxically, some teachers are now (re-)discovering that monolingual English students also benefit from approaches which emphasise language in the curriculum. A teacher from Barking once remarked that bilingual students were the 'barium meal in the system'. They themselves did not constitute a problem, but they showed up all the problems within the education system. One of these problems was that students were expected to make the transition from their everyday experience of using English to using English for academic and cognitive processing by a kind of osmosis rather than through a systematic programme of language development. Despite the Bullock Report (1975) and the subsequent 'language across the curriculum' initiatives, the old attitude that it was the job of the English department to teach 'them' language and the job of the subject teacher to teach Science, History, Geography or whatever, has persisted. Thus, on the one hand there are teachers who effectively ignore the linguistic demands that their subject makes on students whether they are bilingual or monolingual and, on the other, those who recognise that these demands apply in some ways to all their students.

What remains is the issue of how teachers who are aware of the need to take into account the linguistic development of their students can do so effectively within the context of teaching their subject. In the wake of Bullock, subject teachers were often left with little more in the way of strategies than to do more group work, provide spelling lists or correct the students' grammar. Consequently a language-conscious approach sometimes results merely in a 'sandwich' structure whereby some language work is incorporated into the middle of a subject lesson. 'First we'll finish off the work on the Domesday Book and then we'll think about the meanings of some of those words.'

Rather than treat language as a discrete add-on to the subject content, it seems more sensible to think in terms of integrating language and content. The National Curriculum evoked complaints from subject teachers about the lack of time to cover all the required content, still less do language activities. If all lesson activities are simultaneously content focused and language conscious, the issue of time is partially resolved.

More importantly, this notion of integrating language and content begins to address the major question raised in Bullock about the role of language in subject learning. It seems to us that there are four important linguistic dimensions to the integration of language and content

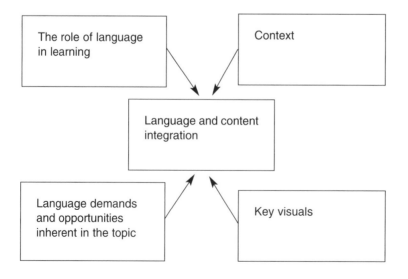

The role of language in learning

Many topics in History and Geography are 'information heavy' and consequently it can be tempting to provide students with large amounts of information and expect them to absorb it. Sometimes information is presented in apparently accessible modes such as teacher explanations, reading aloud from textbooks, videos etc. The assumption that reading textbooks aloud and watching videos make content 'understandable' because it is presented orally and pictorially is not always valid. If teachers feel that the channel of communication (reading) makes understanding difficult, their response may be to avoid reading as much as possible. Similarly, because writing also appears difficult, teachers might demand little more than copying written material or completing worksheets. But avoiding reading and writing is not a viable strategy.

Barnes (1976) characterises a diet of lectures, notes to copy, recall questions etc. as 'transmissional' teaching. The underlying theory of learning postulates the learner as the passive recipient of the knowledge the teacher transmits. What seems critical here though is not so much the predominant channel of communication but what students do with the input. Do students absorb information passively or does it wash over them? Barnes *et. al.* (1971) make the point that:

> It is not that there is too much language, but that it is not fulfilling its functions as an instrument of learning. *Rather, language is seen as an instrument of teaching.* (Original italics)

One consequence of a transmission approach is that students may be able to recall a number of individual facts about a topic but have little understanding of how they relate to the whole topic. Similarly, using a series of worksheets may lead to students acquiring bits of information which have no overall significance for them. The setting of a project can also result in students merely copying pages of (largely unprocessed) information. We can make sense of information by active processing, connecting it with our existing knowledge and fitting it into a mental schema and so acquiring a coherent picture of the facts and their significance. Active learning, therefore, emphasises 'making sense of information'. One important means of making sense is using talk to share and compare (and thereby modify) understandings. Interaction provides the opportunity to express provisional understanding, compare that understanding with other conceptualisations and modify the provisional ideas accordingly.

The partial and fragmented acquisition of knowledge is what Edwards and Mercer (1987) refer to as 'ritual understanding'. They contrast this with 'principled understanding' which is the product of interrogating and processing information.

Barnes *et. al.* directed attention towards the way students could use talk to make sense of input, clarify concepts and grasp meanings. In the last fifteen years or so much has been made of Krashen's concept of 'comprehensible input' in connection with bilingual pupils' acquisition of an additional language (see Dulay, Burt and Krashen, 1982). It has been used to emphasise the importance of concrete referents, visuals and situational context to make the meaning of language input clear to bilingual learners. However, much 'academic' vocabulary cannot be understood in this concrete way because it is essentially abstract in nature and so it is only by exploring meaning through talking around the topic that students can achieve understanding. In effect the 'talking around' provides more 'comprehensible input' with which to work.

Barnes proposed that this exploratory talk could be developed through exploiting the possibilities of small-group tasks which obliged students to use talk in order to achieve a particular goal. But opportunity to participate in a small group does not necessarily lead to exploratory talk. Putting students together in a group can lead to monosyllabic near silence, off-task chat or dogmatic assertion and counter assertion. The opportunity to talk to each other may not be enough to ensure that it contributes to the students' understanding. The implication is that some kinds of talk are more useful than others for supporting learning.

Terry Philips (1985) suggests that there are five modes of on task talk evident in classrooms: the operational mode, the argumentative mode, the expositional mode, the experiential mode and the hypothetical mode.

The operational mode, he suggests, is the kind of talk that accompanies action such as carrying out a practical science experiment. Such talk is relatively inexplicit, relying heavily on the use of pronouns such as 'it' and 'them', general nouns such as 'thing' or 'ones' and deictics such as 'here' and 'there'. It is the kind of talk that is difficult to make sense of unless you can also see what is happening.

In the argumentative mode, as the name suggests, assertion and counter assertion predominate, but justifications are usually inexplicit or become of the 'because I say so' kind.

In the expositional mode the students (or some of them) begin to replicate the kind of teacher-student discourse common when a teacher addresses a whole class. One of the students might take on the task of explaining to others and directing questions. I have even heard students in a small group begin to use typical teacher responses such as 'well done!' when others in the group contribute.

The experiential mode is that in which students draw on their own experience and offer anecdotes, memories and other snippets of information they consider relevant to the topic. Typically students use phrases like: 'I remember when I was young seeing ...' or 'My mum told me that...' or 'In India I saw...'.

The hypothetical mode is the kind of discourse in which students put forward ideas in a tentative manner. They often use phrases such as: 'It could mean that ....' or 'It might be...' or 'Perhaps it was used for.... ' Philips suggests that this is a process of putting ideas on the table for consideration by others and that it invites responses and elaboration. It encourages justification and clarifying and shaping ideas rather than dogmatic assertion – which differentiates it from the argumentative mode.

Philips maintains that the latter two modes, experiential and hypothetical, are most useful in facilitating students' learning because they offer the greatest opportunity for students to reflect on their own experience and integrate it with the 'new' knowledge they are seeking to make sense of.

So what can be done to ensure that small-group talk takes place at all, is on task and is useful in terms of extending and sharpening students' understanding? Three factors in particular seem to influence whether small group interaction leads to exploratory talk: the level of communication skills the students possess, the social climate of the class and the nature of the group task.

Students' communication skills

Communication skills are largely ignored in educational contexts. The work of Sylvia MacNamara, for example (see MacNamara and Moreton, 1995), highlights the need for students to employ skills such as active listening, paraphrasing, summarising, asking clarifying questions, encouraging etc. within a group, in order to engage in purposeful learning. MacNamara suggests that problems within groups stem from a lack of experience in using such skills and the behaviours and language forms which signal interest in the contributions of others and concern about the dynamics of the group. This means that students can end up in conflict (where some engage in argumentative discourse and others withdraw into silence) not through lack of good intentions but through inability to handle the interactions. In turn, this lack of skill significantly affects the social climate in the class.

The social climate of the classroom

One reaction from teachers to the idea of using small group work in the classroom is that students cannot handle it. This may be due to lack of skills but not doing group work merely avoids the problems in the class by reducing student interaction and replacing it with teacher-directed work and individual worksheets. Classroom activity of this type of may keep a 'lid on it', but the underlying tensions will remain. The development and reinforcement of cliques and the marginalisation of individuals may result, so creating a particularly disadvantageous environment for loners and members of out-groups but also impoverishing the learning environment for members of in-groups. Where in-groups and out-groups are determined along ethnic identities there may be even greater cause for concern. Given that the class is likely to reflect the power relations operating in the school and society as a whole, ethnic minority students are likely to be particularly disadvantaged by a lack of cohesion within the class. The end result is that the students in most need of a supportive and positive learning environment are the ones who are most disadvantaged.

The nature of the group task

Group tasks need to encourage participation. Too many are in effect tasks which invite not group interaction but individual action. Tasks may be too unfocused – the instruction to 'get into groups and discuss the poem' can leave the students unclear about how they should conduct the discussion and indeed why they are having a discussion at all. No set of materials placed before students can guarantee their participation, but it helps if they:

- have a clear outcome and goal for the students

- are designed so that discussion is the means of achieving the goal

- have a shared set of objects, cards etc. for the group to manipulate

- are structured so that if necessary students can be provided with procedural protocols (turn taking etc.) or linguistic protocols (This card says.... and I think that's an economic factor. What do you think, Rina?)

- are sufficiently cognitively challenging to be worth collaborating on.

The linguistic demands and opportunities inherent in the topic

Cummins' (1984) hypothesis that there are essentially two types of language, BICS (Basic Interpersonal Communication Skills) and CALP (Cognitive Academic Language Proficiency) has been significant in drawing attention to the nature of the linguistic demands made by the curriculum. In particular it has alerted teachers to the fact that fluent and flexible use of English in social and transactional situations (the playground, the dinner queue, etc.) does not necessarily equip students to use academic English. Cummins maintains that whereas for a beginner bilingual a degree of fluency in BICS tends to be acquired relatively quickly – between one and two years – acquisition of CALP to a level comparable to a monolingual peer of similar ability is more likely to take five to seven years. These finding have been supported by the work of others such as Collier (1989) and Wong Fillmore (1991).

Failure to make the distinction between everyday English and academic English often results in negative observations about students' abilities. 'Her English is OK, it's just that she's not very bright', may be the response to a bilingual pupil struggling to acquire and use academic English. Academic use of English is unlikely to be acquired unless it is explicitly taught. The recognition that CALP-type language is by and large significantly different from BICS-type language in many respects, for example that it is formal, more dense, largely written rather than spoken and more precise, obliges us to consider:

- What barriers to learning does the relative unfamiliarity of academic language put in the way of students?

- How can we plan learning activities which make students more familiar with academic language so that it becomes a tool rather than a barrier to learning?

Linguistic demands

In recent years much attention has been given to the notion of analysing the linguistic demands inherent in topics. Although there have been interesting explorations of language functions and structures in topics (see Levine, 1996 and Vasquez, 1996), in practice attention is focused on topic vocabulary. However, it is not topic specialist vocabulary that causes problems of comprehension but rather how this vocabulary fits into discourse and the structure of different kinds of texts. Students' difficulties are not simply over individual items of vocabulary but with connecting them with other items and using them in extended discourse.

Teachers do need to recognise what vocabulary, structures and discourse features make comprehension more difficult and mediate these demands in the light of analysis. The response may be to provide simplified texts rather than avoid reading altogether. This might well be a useful practice, but it begs the question of what is being simplified in a text. Is it the content or only the language, or both? In simplifying the language might teachers inadvertently simplify the content? If the content is 'simplified' will it be actually more comprehensible? Shortening sentences and texts causes the meaning to become more condensed and the text to have more ellipsis and substitution and fewer connectives. In fact simplifying a text often requires it to be made more explicit and therefore longer.

Opportunities for language development

In planning for bilingual pupils the focus is often on language demands and trying to mediate them. But it seems just as important to make sure that the language opportunities inherent in a topic are exploited. For example, in a topic where cause and effect relations are a significant element it may be appropriate to build practice in using expressions of cause and effect (eg. 'results in', 'leads to', 'is due to') into learning activities. Although the language of interactive oral activities is somewhat unpredictable it can be to some extent anticipated by including specific terms in the task.

It is perhaps easier to include these items in written activities. Controlled and guided writing tasks and 'writing frames' (see Lewis and Wray, 1995) allow students to focus on particular language features. Writing frames are especially useful for supporting students' use of discourse features and appropriate structuring of texts.

Context

Another principle underpinning our planning was that students need cognitively challenging activities. We were concerned that students might:

- be offered challenging input but be required to do little more than copy it or respond to literal questions

- be given input which required undemanding types of thinking such as naming, identifying, repeating etc.

- be offered demanding input and activities but with little support.

Although it is desirable for students to encounter demanding material and activities requiring 'higher order thinking', the answer is not to make the work difficult and hope for the best. Making the curriculum accessible has often been interpreted as a process of simplifying or watering down content and using worksheets. Cummins' quadrant (see Cummins, 1996) provides an alternative way of looking at this issue.

Experience suggests that the difficulty students find with different types of thinking depends on the context in which that thinking is deployed. For example, a student who works on a market stall at weekends may carry out quite complex addition, subtraction and multiplication operations in the course of taking payment and giving change but might get stuck on similar problems when they are decontextualised in a Maths textbook. On the other hand, some less demanding thinking might prove fairly inaccessible because of the unfamiliarity (or abstract nature) of the context. Cummins argues that demanding types of thinking can be offered to students, provided that they are presented initially in a context-embedded situation. This allows students to build on what they already know and to move from the familiar to the context-reduced end of the continuum.

By cognitively challenging activities we mean activities that oblige students to use demanding thinking skills such as hypothesising, classifying, inferring as well as the less demanding ones such as naming, identifying, describing. Activities requiring students to tackle such thinking is important not only to retain educational rigour but also because cognitively undemanding tasks would ultimately restrict students' range of language experiences and prevent their continued language development. Context embedding effectively helps to make the language of the input more comprehensible. Access to the curriculum becomes not a matter of watering down content but of mediating the language demands through contextualising the language of the input.

The successful contextualisation of a learning activity will depend not only on the materials themselves but also on how these are used. Even the finest materials, if used in a way which ignores or undermines what students can bring to the task in terms of their linguistic and cultural experience and their knowledge of the world, are unlikely to engage them. Equally, without frameworks or examples that connect with students' experiences, interacting with each other will seldom enable them to move their thinking and understanding forward. What is needed is both supportive materials and the creation of a supportive environment for using them.

Key visuals

'Key Visuals' is a term used by Bernard Mohan in his book *Language and Content* (1986) to define tables, charts, maps, diagrams, Venn diagrams, time lines and so on which are not just visual aids but essentially 'information packages' which present information in a largely graphical rather than verbal form.

As well as summarising a 'piece of information' they also show the structure of the information. This can be illustrated by considering a text relating a series of events and a time line summarising those events. From a distance the text looks like any page of writing, whereas you would be able to see from the shape of the time line that it detailed a series of events in chronological order. In the same way branching diagrams show the nature of a classification, a map shows the spatial relationship between places, a tick chart shows contrasts in properties or features between two or more things, and so on.

There is a difference between 'visual support' and key visuals. Visual support (a picture of something, an illustration of an action, an object, a puppet, a mime, a video sequence etc.) serves to illustrate particular items of vocabulary. A key visual, on the other hand, is a representation of conceptual relationships between objects, events or situations. Thus a picture of some wheat illustrates the word 'wheat' whereas a calendar diagram might show the temporal relationship between the different stages of cultivation.

Summarising the content in the form of a key visual can be useful for three reasons. Firstly, it is useful for checking the structure and coherence of the content. If the content cannot be successfully represented by a key visual it suggests that it is incoherent in some way, perhaps too vague or possibly incomplete. Gaps in the key visual, e.g. blank cells in a table, alert us to the fact that there is missing information.

Another reason for using a key visual is that it allows us to ask important questions about the amount and nature of the content. Figure 1 on page 90 is a planning key visual relating to land use in Italy.

Using this diagram to think about planning brings into focus questions such as:

- do we want the pupils to know all of this information? If not, what do we want them to know and why?

- is it too detailed/ not detailed enough?

- should there be more/ fewer headings?

Thirdly, key visuals allow teachers to identify more easily both the kinds of thinking and the kinds of language pupils will need in order to explore and verbalise the content. By using key visuals to generate sentences, teachers can investigate both the meanings students need

Figure 1: Land use in Italy

	Area A	Area B	Area C	Area D	Area E
Relief	Mainly flat apart from land around old volcanoes and Vesuvius	Fairly flat	Fairly flat	Fairly flat	Steep limestone hills and cliffs
Soil	Fertile soils where ash and lava from volcanoes have weathered	Soil not important as land is built up	Soil not important as land is built up	Soil not important as land is built up	Thin soil not very fertile
Settlement	Dispersed settlement but fairly densely populated because soil is fertile	Nucleated with high density of population	Nucleated around around factories and port	Linear development along the coast, quite densely populated	Nucleated in coastal resort, otherwise very dispersed
Land use	Small farms, intensive farming of fruit and vegetables	Housing, retail and commercial buildings	Factories and port facilities	Housing, hotels, tourist facilities	Housing and tourist facilities in resorts and some farming on hillside terraces
Jobs	Farming	Commercial, retail and administration	Factory jobs, shipping and fishing	Some retail and tourism related jobs	Tourism related jobs, some retail and farming

to understand and also the form of words they need to express those meanings.

Thus for the example above, it is possible to generate sentences such as:

In area C the settlement is nucleated around the port and factories.

Most of the jobs in area E are concerned with tourism, but there are some jobs concerned with farming and retail.

In area D the land is mostly used for housing, hotels and tourist facilities.

> The soil in area A is fertile, whereas in the soil in area E is thin and not very fertile.

If the end result of an activity is for students to produce a piece of writing then the writing demands of this particular form and content become apparent.

Key visuals can be used to write texts for students. They allow the information content to be retained while the language and structure of the text can be mediated to take into account the students' language and literacy levels. So when simplifying a text, a key visual becomes a useful guide for writing the text and checking it for coherence and completeness.

In addition key visuals can support classroom activities. If the learning activity obliges students to move between text and key visual – verbalising graphical information and visualising verbal information – opportunities are created for them to explore meaning and experiment with ways of putting those meanings into words. Activities can involve students in 'reconstructing' or completing a key visual to explore its information content and structure by verbalising possibilities. In other words the key visual invites discussion of the content and also provides a framework for discussion.

Thus key visuals can be the focus for purposeful activity which can involve and include all children in a mixed experience, multilingual classroom.

A practical example

The example is taken from a unit of work we planned for a Year 9 Geography class on The European Union and the study of one EU Member State. The Department had decided that all staff would use Italy as the Member State which the students would study.

The class involved was a mixed ability Year 9 class of 30 students of whom none was new to English although most needed work to extend their receptive and active vocabularies and develop their ability to extract and organise information from texts and present information in writing. We also wanted to enable the students to develop their skills in making inferences from verbal and graphical data and enhance their geographical skills.

In addition to the linguistic and cognitive aspects of learning we also identified a need for the students to break established patterns of being rather passive learners and operating in the classroom in relatively exclusive groups that left some individuals isolated and others locked into various cliques. These dynamics limited the students' learning. Some had few opportunities to interact and share and compare their ideas, while others were prone to interact rather superficially within their cliques and the bounds of established patterns of social relations. We thought that this passivity in learning and the relatively closed nature of the social relations within the class were linked and decided that setting interactive tasks in random groupings might solve both problems. We also wanted to support their communication skills and realised we needed to model some of these in our own interventions and use 'protocols' for activities.

Planning activities

This section of The European Union and Italy unit was concerned with identifying and locating eight regions of Italy and describing the landscape, climate and economy of each region.

People seem to assume that collaborative learning tasks and the accompanying materials are the result of creative inspiration. In fact, they are generally the product of careful analysis of the learning involved and the context in which it can be most effectively situated. A diagrammatic version of this process is shown below.

What do we want the students to learn?

We think that the planning needs to start with the subject or topic content. This may sound obvious, but lesson content is sometimes driven by other considerations. In response to the topic 'The Regions of Italy' some teachers may say:

'I want them to do some writing. What can they write about?'

'There's a double page spread in the text-book. We can use that.'

'There's a video on it. They can watch that and answer some questions.'

So content may be determined by prior decisions about lesson activities and resources, instead of the activities and resources being

Planning Process

What do we want the students to learn?

Key Visual
How can we summarise the content to be learnt and show the structure of the knowledge in the form of a Key Visual

Language
What language forms do the students need to be able to use to explore and understand the content and therefore 'reconstruct the Key Visual?

Thinking
What kinds of thinking are involved in exploring and understanding the content and the structure of the content?

Context
What elements will activate students' existing knowledge and help them to connect this with the new knowledge?

Activity
What type of activity reflect the kinds of thinking involved in exploring the content?

Exploratory activity
What activity will get students to explore and understand the content and so reconstruct the Key Visual?

Consolidation activity
What activity will enable students to apply and consolidate the learning as generated by the Key Visual?

Language for expressing and applying knowledge of content
What language forms are needed to express the meaning encoded in the Key Visual?

selected according to their relevance to the content. The resources available to teachers are certainly important in determining what can be done in the classroom but that does not mean that they should determine content. Unless teachers are specific about the learning it is difficult to:

- see what conceptual difficulties may lie in the content

- determine the language demands of the content

- establish contexts which activate pupils' existing knowledge.

When the content is specific – 'I want them to know what the regions of Italy are, where they are located and what their climate is like. I also want them to know about their main industries, including tourism' – it becomes easier to see what kinds of thinking the pupils need to do in order to understand the topic and what language they need to explore and express their understanding of the topic. Thus:

identifying ('That must be Sicily....')

cause and effect ('The hot dry summers mean that you can grow citrus fruits......')

describing ('The average rainfall is below 80mm...')

inferring ('That suggests that the land there is more fertile.')

In making decisions about content a number of questions are taken into account either explicitly or implicitly, such as:

- what does the National Curriculum actually say?

- what do the students already know?

- what part of this topic do we want to cover at this stage?

- how will what the students learn now affect future learning in this topic area?

- do we ourselves fully understand the information and concepts involved?

Key visual – how can we summarise the content and show the structure of the knowledge in the form of a key visual?

We use key visuals to check the coherence and completeness of the content, so for the Regions of Italy activity the key visual was a table (produced here in part):

	Location	Landscape	Climate	Industry and farming	Tourist activities
Adriatic Riviera	North-east coast	Sandy beaches	Warm throughout the year, hot in summer. Rainfall below 80mm per month except November	Tourism, fishing	Beaches, cafes, nightclubs, fishing trips
. . .	. . .	. . .	. . .	. . .	. . .
Sicily	Island west of the 'toe' of Italy	Interior high and rocky, coastal areas flatter with sandy beaches	Warm all year but hot and dry in summer. Some rain in winter	Citrus fruit and olives. Fruit processing and canning factories	Beaches, Mount Etna, nature reserve

When we looked at this we were aware that it contained a good deal of information so the students would need to deal with a lot of source material if they were to 'reconstruct' it. Consequently we decided that it would be sensible for students initially to research only two of the regions rather than all eight. However, we saw the possibility here for different groups of students to research a different pair of regions and become expert groups. The expert groups could then be 'jigsawed' so that each new group contained four experts on different pairs of regions who could then share their information on all eight regions with each other. In this way we thought that student would gain experience in:

- extracting information from text

- recording relevant information systematically

- listening to, receiving and recording information from others

- giving and explaining information to others

- organising themselves and others to achieve a common goal

The series of activities

Activity 1: *Reading, locating relevant information and recording it.* Each group was given two texts and a table. The table had headings for location, landscape, industry, and farming and tourism and left space for information about each of the eight regions. The texts were passages in continuous prose about the regions. The students' task was to locate relevant information in their text and summarise it in the appropriate cell in the table, so re-constructing the Key Visual and moving from a primarily verbal form to a partly visual form.

Activity 2: *Matching written description of climate to climate graph.* We gave the students eight climate graphs corresponding to each of the eight regions. Their task was to decide which two graphs showed the climate for their regions, using information from their texts. Again the students were being asked to move 'forwards and back-wards' between the verbal and graphical descriptions of the climate and establish a correspondence between these two forms. In each group the students' texts had been marked A, B, C or D. 'Jigsawing' was achieved when the As, Bs, Cs and Ds in each half of the class formed new groups of four.

Activity 3: *Sharing information orally, recording information on the table and checking that climate graphs were correctly matched to regions.*
The class were re-grouped so that each new group had students with expert information on 'their' regions. They now had to share the information about their two regions so that each member of the group could fill in the missing information on their table. Each student completed the original key visual and could then explain which graph went with which region. If any of the initial groups had not made a correct decision it would come to light at the point when two students claimed the same graph for their regions. Any dispute led to a return to the texts to justify decisions. In the end the correct matchings were worked out.

Activity 4: *Matching eight 'typical' photographs to each of the eight regions.*

Students now matched eight photographs to each of the regions in order to bring together their overall impressions by deciding which picture contained 'typical' elements of the area. The students made comments such as:

'Picture B could be Sicily because it looks pretty dry.'

'The South has hills and is dry.'

'That looks like they're growing rice, so it could be the North-East.'

Activity 5: *Deciding which region eight fictitious families should visit for their holidays.*

We wanted students to apply their knowledge of the regions to a practical problem and so develop their ability to use inference. Consequently we devised a task in which eight families were going to visit Italy for a holiday Each family had different interests and requirements and the students had to match each family to the most suitable region. To achieve this the students had to read some information about each family and infer what region would suit them. They had to complete a table showing which region the family should visit and what weather was likely in August. This is another example of a task which effectively asks student to re-construct a key visual by interpreting and reorganising the verbal information.

Activity 6: *Writing a postcard home from one of the families.*

The final activity was to choose one of the families and write a postcard from a member of the family. This was a way of getting students to summarise information about one of the regions. In order to provide support for writing the postcard and to ensure that it became an effective summary of the region, we provided a 'writing frame'

We hoped that this series of activities would give students the opportunity to make sense of the regions of Italy in terms of the relationships between location, landscape and climate. For example, if they were noticing differences between the dry, hot, south of Italy and the mountain region with a more extreme climate this would show some measure of understanding.

The planning process is not a rigid agenda for planning but a flexible tool for helping teachers to understand more about the language and learning demands of the curriculum. Mainstream and language specialist teachers have found that it has led to the development of a 'common language' to analyse content and language and so plan learning activities which are effective for all students.

7
Planning for inclusion; learning at Key Stage 4
Dympna MacGahern and Kwaku Boaten

The general school context

The lessons outlined in this chapter took place in a large, nine-form entry comprehensive school for girls in North London. The school is distinctive for its broad range of ethnicity and languages since it is the only girls' school in the Borough and draws its students from seventy-two feeder primary schools and from a wide social spectrum. The school is 57% multilingual and 78% of pupils are from ethnic minority backgrounds. Sixty different languages are spoken in the school, the largest groups being of Turkish, Bangladeshi and African-Caribbean origin. Individual students speak another thirty languages. There is a sizeable number of refugee students, some with the noticeable needs associated with the trauma of recent experience, some entering Years 9 and 10 with little or interrupted prior schooling and all in considerable academic and social need. There is high student mobility and 35% of the pupils are entitled to free school meals.

Although the school has no policy for language across the curriculum, it does have one on bilingualism and a strong equal opportunities policy. Mainstream staff are keen to work with teachers funded by the Ethnic Minority and Travellers Achievement Grant (EMTAG) and there is a system whereby Heads of Department indicate areas for development and request input from the team. Dissemination of strategies and materials has been a feature of work jointly undertaken between subject departments and the EMTAG department.

The achievement of bilingual students, particularly in relation to their inability to express in English what they know, as demanded by the public exam system, is under constant consideration. While issues of language development are generally well aired and likely to be fairly familiar, issues of cultural inclusivity feature less in schemes of work than they did before the implementation of the National

Curriculum. The statutory nature of the National Curriculum encourages a timidity, even conservatism in interpreting the Orders, thereby reinforcing the ethnocentric base of most teachers' own educational experience.

The sessions described were planned by the EMTAG teacher but both teachers were present during the lesson and participated throughout. The effect of the 'warm-up' lesson was to authorise full participation by all from the outset. In London 'issues' sometimes become polarised as the groups adopt distancing techniques – *'it's about black and white'*; *'it's not about us'*; *it's about refugees'*; *'it's about being bilingual'*. This behaviour is not unique to students. It is also observable at teacher and institution level.

English is a core subject for all the 27 students in the class, which has a representative cross-section of the school population. Ten students, five black and five white, were monolingual, four were bilingual competent users of English and ten at differing stages of English language acquisition and expected to cope with the various linguistic demands this implies. Three students were early stage learners of English.

This is a school which generally expects race issues to be discussed openly with students: it was difficult not to, since this was the time of the crippling attack on Qudus Ali in Whitechapel and the murder of Stephen Lawrence in Eltham. The existence of societal racism is a tangible fact of life for London youth – they can arrive in school visibly upset because a racist (mostly, but not always white) adult has verbally abused them on the bus. Anything can invite the assault – their colour, but also their dress, hair, quiet demeanour or feistiness. Racist bullying can happen in school. Racism between students is dealt with strictly but subtle and institutional racism often goes unrecognised except by the victims. Both white and black students are very aware of this and of how pervasive it is. But although it is readily admitted to be grossly unfair, there is a sense among the young people that they themselves can do little to change things.

Preparing to read a 19th Century short story

The text to be studied by Year 10 was a 19th Century short story, *Desiree's Baby* by Kate Chopin. The central issue of this short story is historical racism. Set in the Southern United States, it has a slave-owning plantation family of French background as the main protagonists. A young woman of uncertain origin marries the plantation owner and produces a 'quadroon' heir. Her consequent suicide is as controversial as the denouement which reveals the plantation owner is himself of 'tainted' blood. *Desiree's Baby* is a cocktail of historical negative race constructs with considerable potential to damage both white and black young students by apparently legitimising offensiveness.

Previously the introduction to the text was a 'cold' first read by student volunteers and the teacher, with some commentary by the teacher to help contextualise and elucidate. In the course of the detailed study of the text inevitably historical attitudes to race and gender would have been exposed and examined but the immediate question was: what would the impact be of the planned 'cold' and shocking first read? Black parents have often told us about the negative effect on their children of teaching about white cruelty to black victims.

Accordingly a warm-up was designed for the lesson through a set of true/false statements around the subject of world slavery. The discussion generated by the statements was planned so the class could counterbalance the image of black people as victims with facts about survival, courage, dignity, creativity and serious public roles.

Students were asked to work collaboratively to check their knowledge of world slavery by deciding whether the following statements were true or false:

                                                              True/False

1. There are millions of slaves in the world today

2. White people were never enslaved

3. There was a slave trade in white European women last century

4. There are no slaves in London today

5. Only white people helped to emancipate (get freedom for) black slaves in the Southern States of America

6. In the period of enslavement in the Southern States, there was no inter-racial mixing (social, political, sexual)

7. Black people had no position of influence or power in Europe at the time of slavery

---

With the statements went a supporting teacher information sheet with a sheaf of photographic evidence and other documents derived mainly from recent research (for sources see bibliography), but this was not given to the students until they had made a genuine attempt to engage with the statements. The intention was to stimulate fuller discussion and draw on students' own knowledge and experience by not giving the answers immediately. The picture file therefore became a kind of answer sheet. The visual information contained pictures of young slaves, black and white, contemporaneous to the story and of well known European aristocrats with black ancestry, including a cousin of the present Queen and Queen Charlotte Sophia, grandmother of Queen Victoria.

For most of the students the pictorial evidence was new and surprising. As part of the learning objectives of the lesson the teacher needed to ensure that students understood that this social history had not been fully or accurately documented until recently, so that fiction sometimes came closer to reality. There has always been social, political and sexual interaction between different ethnic groups, as evidenced in the picture file.

Presenting the lesson

The lesson was presented to the students as preparation for an exercise in detecting bias in the story. It aimed to show how the status quo contained or declared its bias and to develop students' own critical and analytical powers. This was a step away from traditional English Literary Criticism which at Key Stage 4 generally invites students to empathise with the characters, atmosphere, emotions and settings portrayed. Here students faced a simpler but possibly more challenging consideration of comparatively unknown aspects of history, put to the service of contextualising a19th Century fiction text. It was one brief experience for the students of challenging what they read in print and learning to 'read' the omissions. While empathy and the language which generates empathy are legitimate learning fields, there is equally a need to raise issues around: the writer's point of view, evidence from the written word of the social and historical angle on race and gender and audience awareness and response.

So that students could verify the true/false statements, they were given the teacher information sheet. This included the information that even today domestic slaves, mainly from the Philippines and Bangladesh live in rich London households. This was painful for the one shy, bright, middle class Filipino student and the sizeable Bengali group. We had considered the possibility of toning down such unpalatable facts and whether they should they be suppressed because of group sensitivities but eventually we decided to opt for accuracy and openness.

On the true/false statements information was given that '*there was a slave trade in white European women last century*'. Students learned that in Britain there was a spate during the last century of drugging poor women so that they could be transported by coffin to Holland and from there to the harems of Turkey and the Middle East. These women were prized possessions in brothels. Such trade has parallels today in major pimping operations based in London that exploit women from Lithuania, Eastern Europe and South America. (Although today's women travel by air instead of in coffins – there is an irony in this flight to the land of opportunity!)

The objective and the response

The task required all the students to understand the effect of treatment that is dehumanising, unjust, psychologically damaging and ultimately life threatening – as the story illustrates. The purpose of the true/false statements and the teacher information pack was overtly to contextualise the racism of *Desiree's Baby* so that the black students would not experience the story reading in terms of victimisation. Students need to know that other vulnerable groups (e.g. women) did and do suffer similar brutalisation and that inferior status is not related only to skin colour but can be based on gender or socio-economic status. As an aside to statement number 5, '*only white people helped to emancipate black slaves in the Southern States of America*', it was also important to establish that the social history of the achievements of black people – scientists, politicians, orators, educationists, artists – though well documented, is only grudgingly being told even now. Consequently the information pack contained biographical details of famous political anti-slavery activists who operated directly against their oppressors: Harriet Tubman, Sojourner Truth, Frederick Douglass, Nanny of the Maroons, Kofi, and others.

The learners brought differing responses to a socially sensitive subject seldom featured in the curriculum, so careful planning and preparation was essential. We surmised that all students were likely to bring an assumption that only black people were enslaved and that slavery is exclusively an historical issue. As it happened, black students displayed a broader understanding of the issues than other groups. There was general awareness of child slavery in Asia today and to some extent also about the existence of Indian and African slaves in certain Arab States. On the subject of white slavery we mentioned the little publicised fact that the Irish were sent as slaves to Montserrat during the time of the main triangular slave trading phase, which is why names like Riley, Dubarry and Murphy remain common family names among Monserrattians and the shamrock is an emblem of the island. One confident student said she now understood why her Montserrattian Grandma claimed to be Irish and there followed a discussion about attitudes to lighter and darker skin tones among members of her family.

Linguistically the students had varying degrees of ability to read, discuss, volunteer information, listen, question and speculate. In terms of their social, cognitive and linguistic development they needed to listen to facts, question, seek clarification and amplification and reason about consequences, and the lesson gave them the opportunity to look at facts and outcomes without attributing blame. They were invited to continue this research by looking through source books and in some cases checking or confirming information with parents or carers.

The issues of mixed race

The issues of racial mixing also needed to feature in the preparation for reading the story since not only the story content but also the language used to tell it was offensive. The term 'quadroon', used to describe somebody one quarter black, is not a word that is familiar to contemporary London students. It carries negative connotations and highlights the way labelling can be used by the dominant group as a form of control. The labelling of people of mixed parentage was relevant to several students in the class. To place 'quadroon' more accurately into its pluralist historical setting, students were asked to list the names they had heard applied to people of mixed heritage. They listed all the derogatory terms commonly used about black people including 'half caste' and 'mixed race'. It seemed appropriate to mention Tiger Woods, a high profile American golfing hero of mixed origins who describes himself as Cablinasian: Caucasian, Black, Indian and Asian. In keeping with the democratic direction of the lesson, students were invited to generate their own positive titling system. They were reminded of places around the globe from which students in the class and their families originated: Mauritius, the Caribbean, Holland, Britain. The picture file was again a useful reference and the 'warm up' lesson became a social history lesson needed for dealing with overt historical racism.

It is interesting to speculate on how a text such as *Desiree's Baby* came to be on the syllabus. It was possibly indicative of a particular decade and mindset, just as Irish history was once considered satisfactorily taught if the Famine was included. Students were taught about the poor, hapless peasants who couldn't withstand the blow of the potato blight. The fact that food was exported from Ireland during most of the famine years was seldom discussed. Students of Irish ancestry cringed or pretended not to be Irish. An inclusive curriculum designed in line with this outlook meant teaching about slavery – since a strenuous curriculum could face such unpalatable facts, particularly when the plight of the victim was the focus. Details and subtleties were for adults. Students of ethnic minority origin detested these lessons. I know this as a teacher and parent.

Indicating how social history might be constructed to the advantage of dominant groups and how existing accounts are biased encouraged critical thinking. The preparatory lesson ensured the story would be read as more than the tale of a passive victim, doomed to cruelty and shame. The social and historical context of the story could itself be scrutinised. Being outraged at the denouement was not enough; the process leading to the denouement also needed questioning and the greatest potential for offensiveness lay in accepting the premise of race and gender superiority in the story.

The sense of outrage felt and expressed by the students at the denouement of the story was palpable, as it would have been for any vocal and informed reader. But airing the issues in advance of the reading demystified some of the events of the story. It also prepared more students for some of the 'unfair' shocks in the text and lessened the perception of such experience as reserved for black people only. Students were able to express outrage rather than just sympathy for the victim. The approach was successful because it gave all students permission to condemn the pernicious, pervasive historical racism of the text. The openness that was created through information and discussion secured honest responses; it allowed students to say whether the racism was historical or whether it described the fragile conditions of today; it lessened the possibility of glossing over the issues as merely historical. The preparatory lesson also gave the students an opportunity to feel more in control when they were invited to work with and on behalf of the students of mixed heritage in order to identify and name the racial groups with whom they felt an affinity. Such activity reduced the wounding potential of a term like 'quadroon' and added contemporary pertinence to the issues.

Lessons in the theory of PE KS4

As part of the unit called *The Organisation of Sport in Britain* three lessons on Finance in Sport were undertaken with Year 11 students studying the Theory of PE for GCSE. As this subject is timetabled against the more popular Drama and Art for Key Stage 4 option choices there is a fairly low take up, so there were only fourteen students in the class. The Head of Department was eager to improve exam results which were poor, she surmised because of the subject's taxing cross-curricular demands comprising Science, Sociology, Maths and Business Studies. This multi-disciplinary character was out of keeping with the barely academic status which the subject had in Key Stage 3. She was concerned that students with practical ability could easily underestimate the difficult theoretical base of the subject. She was also aware, possibly because she had English in her own academic background, of the huge linguistic demands this subject made on students, particularly on bilingual students. We agreed that our aim was to make the subject more linguistically accessible.

The lessons came when exam and revision strategies were a key focus and so we sought make dry factual material not just accessible but also memorable. The lessons were designed to provide an understanding of how money is raised and spent nationally and locally on Sport. Three activities were devised to support these objectives.

The students

The ethnic composition of the class was as varied and the need as wide-ranging as anywhere in the school. There was a newly arrived Kurdish student who joined the class not by choice but because other options were full when she arrived in Year 10. She was literate in Turkish but by the beginning of Year 11 was still in her 'silent' phase. The lessons described provided her with an opportunity to hear discussions about local sport provision with which she was gaining some familiarity. She herself automatically translated key words and phrases into Turkish on her note-taking frame. Occasionally, if directly addressed in Turkish, the other Turkish speaking student would explain in their first language but seemed reluctant to do so routinely. This student needed to develop her academic English, even though her social English and oral competence masked her difficulties. She did not value Turkish as a tool for learning and said that helping the Kurdish student interfered with her own needs. To be fair, her academic Turkish was underdeveloped and she struggled to make her explanations clear.

Although it was school policy that new arrivals were supported by a peer who shared their language if possible, it was also accepted that confident, competent users of English were needed for the induction and support of new students. In this instance the Kurdish student's needs were poorly addressed, as can easily happen in Key Stage 4 which is not as socially coherent as Key Stage 3.

A Somali student who had arrived in Britain in Year 7 was also struggling with academic English. She, however, not only had great personal and social skills but her command of London English, oral and written, gave her enormous peer acceptability. She allied this with a quiet diligence over homework but she had an appetite for classroom gossip (loudly if possible but otherwise quietly and persistently!). The Cantonese speaker who had been British educated was academically and linguistically the most competent student in the group. A Ghanaian student who believed that chunks of text could be learned by rote and regurgitated at exams was impatient with a system of tasks that moved too far from her textbook and would generally want to know where in the text she could find everything that was said. She was very vocal and readily applied the word 'boring' to school in general. Her regular lesson partner was an equally diligent but less book-dominated British Asian of Gujerati-speaking heritage.

The students of African-Caribbean background were as varied as people from any ethnic group: one shy; one quiet, diligent and focused; one practical who, if asked, was able to speak with considerable command and knowledge about her skills and observations on a one-to-one basis but lacked confidence, rarely volunteering to speak in class and presenting poor written work; one was able, bright, analytical, ambitious and focused; another, whose career had been characterised by fairly strenuous and regular struggles with the institution, was outspoken and moody but determined to achieve her GCSE in this subject. The Anglo-Egyptian student was a talker, questioner, prolific note taker and keen to do well. The only white monolingual student was academically able but she too was quite shy and did not readily volunteer to contribute at whole class level.

The learning objectives

In order to engage fully with the collaborative activities, called DARTs (Directed Activities Related to Texts) by Lunzer and Gardner (1984), students needed the social training to value peer collaboration in their use of discussion and problem solving as a way to interpret and consolidate learning. Accordingly, every opportunity was taken to validate the role of oracy in literacy development and learning as an overt, on-going feature of the teaching partnership. All the students readily admitted their need in these respects. They wanted to improve their English as well as their subject knowledge for the forthcoming exams. When designing the lessons we followed our 'hunch' that impressive technical terms borrowed from Local Government, Business Studies or Advertising and widely used in textbooks and exam questions were likely to mask students' nascent knowledge. The teacher's aim was to maximise students' existing knowledge by building on their understanding of how local government works and by following their sporting interests via media coverage. The teacher also needed to encourage students' confidence to use their considerable background knowledge.

The first task (see Figure 1) was an active reading exercise on the details of *The Sources of Finance in Sport*. Students were required to link the source of funds with information on how the money is raised and distributed and the approximate gross annual amount. The information also had a cloze element and the teachers planned

Figure 1: Sources of finance

Finance in Sport   *Work in pairs*

Match each source with its correct detail. Then fill in the missing detail.

Sources of Finance	The detail of how the money is raised and who benefits
1. The Government	Companies give money or other help to athletes, teams or events. Rover ....the tennis school at Bisham Abbey. IBM and ....sponsor the Olympics
2. Local Councils	This raises about £250 million a year for sport (5.6p from each ticket). The money goes into ....Fund and is given out as.........by the Sports Council
3. The National Lottery	..........tickets to events, and replica..........and so on. Big clubs can earn a lot this way
4. TV and radio	Wealthy people may finance their favourite clubs, or even buy them!
5. Sponsorship	These are charged by ....clubs, for example
6. Private individuals	These pay the governing bodies of sport for the right to...............events. In 1995 BSkyB agreed to pay £40 million a year, for 5 years, for ....football matches
7. Tickets and merchandise	They raise money from local taxes and spend some of it on facilities like ....and ....
8. Membership and booking fee	It raises money from taxes. Some goes to sport, through the Department of National Heritage..............gets most of it – around £47 million a year

to be ready to prompt students on how to engage efficiently with the task of scanning a text so that they could complete the sheet rapidly. Groups also needed to be prompted to start at an accessible place since an easy way into a task generates confidence by suggesting achievability. Skim and scan reading techniques were needed for the matching activity: '... *tickets to events, and replica... and so on. Big clubs can earn a lot this way*' evidently linked to 'Tickets and Merchandise'. The cloze dimension rendered the reading more active and required peer discussion. It was therefore likely to become more memorable. As students engaged in the task their eventual overall effectiveness was supported through achievable challenges – not tests.

The second task (see Figure 2) was to provide fuller, even topical illustration from their general knowledge of sources of finance for sport. The purpose of this task was to deepen and broaden understanding through again engaging students' general knowledge. By reading the information on 'how money is raised for sport', students could use their own knowledge and the guidance questions to write notes about taxation, sponsorship and tickets and merchandising, for example. Not all students had all the knowledge required to contribute to this task but collaboration and some (minimal) teacher intervention extended the knowledge base of all students. Here the teacher directed leading questions to known 'enthusiasts' so that for example, tennis, cricket, the London Marathon were cited in answer to the prompt to name 'some other broadcast sport events' other than the one already given. The task gave concrete exemplification of the beneficiaries of the finance discussed in the previous activity and complemented the cloze activity just completed. So students again encountered the statements about the sources of finance together with outline detail for each source thus providing accessible reinforcement for revision.

Supporting Critical Thinking

The approach so far encouraged students to value, incorporate and adapt what they knew to fit a *who does what* frame of reference, at the same time establishing the right to ask *why and how*. The kind of discussion the students engaged in was clearly tied in with current sport news. It also placed the learning within the context of the students' own experiences and encouraged them to question the information and relationships they uncovered. Confident students made open assertions about what they called the 'rigged world of sport'; others listened, approved, challenged or extended with their own examples. All were actively testing what they knew or learning something new. This all-female group discussed the low media profile given to women's sport in general. Someone cited Wimbledon as an important fixture with an historically fairer approach. The object of the lesson was not to debate discrimination in media coverage or even in funding allocation, but to develop the process of note taking, discussion and illustration from students' own experience and to use these to gain a deeper understanding of the criteria for allocating resources, and fairness in sport.

Figure 2: How it's Done

Finance in Sport *Work in pairs*

Discuss and make notes on the questions

Money in from.............
This shows how money is raised for sport

Some questions to discuss a and make notes on

1. The Government. It raises money from taxes. Some goes to sport, through the Department of National Heritage. The Sports Council gets most of it – around £47 million a year.

Who might National Heritage give money to?

2. Local Councils. They raise money from local taxes and spend some of it on facilities like swimming pools, playing fields and school gyms

Name some ways of raising local tax

3. The National Lottery. This raised about £250 million a year for sport (5.6p from each ticket). The money goes into the Lottery Sports Fund and is given out as grants by the Sports Council

Do you know of any sport activity sponsored by the National Lottery?

4. TV and radio. These pay the governing bodies of sport for the right to broadcast sports events. In 1995 BSkyB agreed to pay £40 million a year for 5 years, for Premier League football matches

Name some other broadcast sport events

5. Sponsorship. Companies give money or other help to athletes, teams or events. Rover sponsors the tennis school at Bisham Abbey. IBM and Coca Cola sponsor the Olympics

List some other sponsors or other sports that you know

6. Private individuals. Wealthy people may finance their favourite clubs, or even buy them! Rovers is owned by the millionaire Jack Walker

Name any wealthy owners of a sports club or sport facility that you know

7. Ticket and merchandise. Clubs sell tickets to events and replica kit, scarves, flags and so on. Big clubs can earn a lot this way

What's your favourite merchandise – what do you know about sport's influence on fashion?

8. Membership and booking fees. These are charged by golf and squash clubs, for example

Name any clubs you know that charge membership. (Do you know how much they raise through this? The answer is only a phone call away!)

The more that learning encourages students to ask questions, the more genuinely informed they become beyond the limited, practical requirements of examinable knowledge. Students might think that social or economic structures are set and immutable, and the way certain sports are sponsored or allocated central Government controlled funds can appear to support such a view. They might assume that rote knowledge of '*who*' and '*what*' facts constitutes knowledge and are what is required, while '*how*' and '*why*' questions are reserved for advanced stages of study. Such a view of teaching and learning disadvantages students, particularly bilingual students and those who lack self-confidence. Throughout their schooling they might not have felt confident to express their views because of lack of fluency in English or lack of confidence in their own knowledge or fear of having their contributions marginalised and ignored. Over their school life they might have learned to suppress or undervalue the questioning process that is part of thinking. A teaching approach which aims to transmit facts only, without reasoning and questioning, can at best support a transmission rather than an enquiry based model of learning.

Valuing general knowledge and prior learning

Students also discussed, with great expertise, youth fashion and sport merchandising. They were keenly aware of sponsors' high profit margins and their role in promoting or ignoring particular sports. Generally the students gave uncritical approval to the consumer dream world of star players, which they attributed to well earned, hard won reward for skill. They showed detailed knowledge of their heroes' earning capacity and the sources of such finance – players are part of pop culture. The biographical profiles of sporting celebrities are part of their knowledge, which students eagerly insert into the drier regions of their course. Their heroes are sometimes engaged in acrimonious disputes that make the headlines. Such wrangling over money has considerable educational value, is avidly followed and generally clearly understood by students. It is a readily available resource and humanises otherwise arid theoretical fields. Providing opportunities to share such insights is at the heart of planning for learning which is accessible, challenging and extends understanding of how society operates.

Culture specific references

Textbooks written for exams all have core course content references that are culture-specific. In the context of the theory of PE, where these lessons were lodged, there were references to the National Heritage, National Lottery and the Sports Council. Students drew on their broader knowledge derived not just from study of the syllabus but from magazines, television and personal interests. National Heritage is a particularly inaccessible cultural reference, unfamiliar to many inner city students. The teacher's role was to recognise that this was a stumbling block to understanding and find a way to both localise and cross-reference information about it. There is a small local history museum in a castle nearby which students probably visited in primary school – if they went to a local primary school. It bore the National Heritage symbol and the teacher was able to link this building and its symbol with the Leisure (if not specifically Sport) Industry. To reinforce this connection a question about who takes care of coastal paths was cross-referenced to Geography or Environmental Studies.

The final task

The final task again drew heavily on students' general knowledge, requiring them to show understanding about how sporting concerns communicate, publicise, advertise, improve facilities, respond to need or extend provision. Broad categories were provided on a note-taking grid sheet (see Figure 3) for how the money for sport is spent e.g for *developing the sport, building and improving facilities, prize money* etc. The students had to discuss and record on the note-taking frame for each of the broad categories: *who might spend the money, why this money should be spent and what kinds of things would be done.*

To do this they needed to understand the basic business principles behind the expenditure and to think in terms of sustaining, maintaining, expanding, promoting, organising and managing sport. Again students had to be willing to share their knowledge, speculate about and interpret information, and understand how local activity mirrors as well as meshes with larger-scale national operations. They needed to draw on their local knowledge of sport facilities and requirements to provide illustrations of the broad reasons for how and why money is expended on sport. A local authority might need

Figure 3: How the money is spent

Finance in Sport *Work in Pairs*

The broad categories on how the money for sport is spent:

1. developing the sport

2. building and improving facilities

3. training athletes at all levels

4. training coaches, referees and umpires

5. running events of all sizes

6. the salaries of paid officials and other employees

7. the salaries of professional players

8. prize money

9. sports scholarships

10. day-to-day running expenses

11. payments to shareholders where a club is a limited company

Use the Grid to give examples of –   Who might spend the money
why the money should be spent
what it should be spent on

Category	Who might spend the money?	Why the money should be spent	What it should be spent on
1.			
2.			
3.			

to re-surface the base of a swimming pool for health and safety reasons, while a club owner might expand gym facilities to respond to demand created by an advertising campaign. Initially students needed encouragement to draw on their range of knowledge of local facilities to support their extended understanding of the issues relating to Finance in Sport.

Frames support literacy development and revision

In the final note-taking frame students could recognise the usefulness of charts and notes to summarise, present, organise and record examinable information. They needed to recognise that the notes, derived collaboratively in discussion to which they had contributed, were also an effective revision technique. In these lessons, previously disregarded knowledge was brought to bear on important facts. Half-remembered detail was filled out, memory was activated and rounded through educationally valid means while salient points from all the lessons were recorded on a note-taking frame. Again the teacher needed to encourage ownership of the grid and reassure the students that gaps were acceptable. They illustrated strengths and weaknesses and mapped the reality of the state of student knowledge and the purpose of the task. This final task presented an ideal opportunity to 'jigsaw' so that 'experts' could provide illustrations of missing items. Once every working group had made an attempt to complete the grid they could share their knowledge so that all students had a full version of it.

The lessons outlined were simple in design and purpose. They recognised the interplay and interdependence of social, cognitive and linguistic skills. Teachers explicitly shared the process and purpose of the lesson with the students. Through this process exams became less alarming and more of an opportunity to display what students knew. This was achieved by encouraging them to recognise themselves and each other as a valid sources of knowledge and information. It is through such activity that confidence is built and learning is contextualised in the familiar. Social skills, including using language orally by naming, recalling, narrating and describing are employed to promote social, linguistic and cognitive development, and social skills, knowledge and learning are examined through the public examination system.

Language Support in Design and Technology at Key Stage 4
Partnership Teaching and the DT Department

English as an Additional Language provision in the school is delivered in partnership with departments. Departments request language support for a particular project or unit of work they have planned. It is a requirement of the partnership that the language support teacher and the subject teacher plan the lesson together and share classroom management and marking. Planning is crucial because it allows both teachers to discuss underlying assumptions, including those about language, in the design and delivery of the lesson.

The partnership itself is evaluated from time to time and particularly at the end of each project. The partnership model is also a way of providing INSET to colleagues about language development in the learning and teaching process so that mainstream teachers can continue to support students' language development and learning. At Key Stage 4 the Design and Technology Department work on a project basis and according to a format which consists of identifying a need (by researching what is already available), producing a design brief that includes investigation, specifications, design ideas, through to the final idea, development, making and evaluation. The plan is that by the end of Key Stage 3 students should already be familiar enough with this format to generate their own design brief and move through the stages with increasing independence and confidence.

Even at early stages of developing English, students have a considerable amount of passive vocabulary and show signs of literacy awareness – interest in print, awareness of the English alphabet, emergent reading and writing. During the process of language acquisition this knowledge and awareness can be tapped, for example through brainstorming.

Each stage of the format imposes its own unique language demands and encourages the students to think, create, describe, explain and evaluate their own experience This means that each section can be a deliberate focus for language development. Students and teachers take on different roles throughout the process and each carries its own set of language demands. For example, when identifying a need students could be using language such as: 'My research has shown....' 'I found that...' During the second phase of specifications concerning aesthetic and ergonomic considerations they might use phrases such as: 'My game should...'. The drawing and annotations will include language like: 'It is made of...', 'They have got...' or 'It is easy to play...'. In the making mode the teacher assumes the role of consultant offering the more experienced students supervision, support and advice. But for students at an early stage of learning English the making phase also reveals their prior educational experience. They may be experienced in handling and controlling tools and equipment. They may need the vocabulary of measurement, dimensions etc. in devising their 'cutting list'. Terms for shaping, such 'cutting', 'sawing', 'sanding' and 'smoothing' can provide the opportunity for the teacher to illustrate and model appropriate descriptive vocabulary and to match the tools with their functions. In this way the work of the language support department and the subject teacher complement each other to the benefit of the student.

The lesson

The lesson described here was intended to launch a piece of GCSE coursework. Students had to design and make an entertaining and educational game for an age group of their choice. The general statement of aims of the SEG examining board reads, 'Design and technology requires candidates to combine their designing and making skills with knowledge and understanding.' (SEG Examining Board, GCSE Syllabus for 2001, S01/57). The discussion in this paper applies to Graphics as it is the element for which I originally designed the programme, although it is clearly applicable to other elements too.

Target students: There are altogether seven students in early (but different) stages of developing English, all with different mother tongues. The Czech and Turkish speakers, both recent arrivals, are at stage 1. A Somali student is at stage 2 and four others, three Turkish and one Chinese, are at stage 3. All except the Somali girl are literate in their mother tongues and one of the Turkish speakers is also bilingual and biliterate in Greek. We accept students' own claims to literacy in the mother tongue because the school does not have the resources to assess these claims except for Turkish and some of the Asian languages. The Chinese and Somali students are both keen and committed and talk to share ideas without inhibition. The other students are open to support from a teacher or one another, but are less dynamic. The Somali girl has now confided to me that she can speak neither her mother tongue nor Arabic, her second language, properly on account of disruption to her life. She is literate in neither.

The students are given the aim of identifying a need for their game. The first stage of investigating the design brief is to play a game chosen from a supply of available board games. This activity generates plenty of talk and allows the rules of playing and turn-taking to be modelled. After playing, the particular attributes of the game are identified, on the board or on paper, so that students can focus their investigations and also use them as prompts in writing up this aspect of their design brief. Students were given a grid of possible attributes which they could tick or refer to and keep for later.

Attributes	Characteristics
Shape	Square ☐ Triangle ▽
Look	Attractive, colourful
Kind of game	Board game
Number of players	

When another bilingual student can act as translator the vocabulary can be written in other languages to facilitate the investigation. Otherwise, if the student is literate in her mother tongue, she can use a bilingual dictionary for key vocabulary. Students who are not literate in their mother tongue will be able to copy from the grid. In all cases, drawing and annotation are emphasised as important aspects of language development.

With the teacher as a guide students can use a substitution table, such as the one below, to construct appropriate sentences about the game they have played. Initially the teacher might ask a more fluent speaker of English, 'What game did we investigate?' The answer could then be rephrased as a complete sentence, as appropriate for later explanatory writing, and set in the substitution table.

I			Monopoly
We	investigated		Snakes and Ladders
Karolina	played		Scrabble
Uma	researched		chess
She			

Each stage of the process needs to be accompanied by annotated drawings and other images such as pictures, sample packaging etc. At this stage the emphasis is on familiarisation with sentence structures through modelling and oral and aural practice. The illustrations are used to illuminate meaning and for the student to record and present her investigations. Annotations may also be supported by phrases and sentences from substitution tables.

The pieces	are	made of	wood
They	is	in	plastic
The board			fabric
			paper
			different colours

When the game has been played, the characteristics recorded and the annotated drawings made, the student is ready to use the more detailed substitution tables to record all her findings. Again the teacher might ask the question 'What did we find out about Snakes and Ladders in our investigation?' and set the answer in the form of a substitution table.

I	discovered	that	Monopoly		has got	four pieces
Uma	found		Snakes and Ladders		has	pictures on it
Karolina	learned		chess			money with it
We	noticed					
She						

At each stage the teacher and/or translator would need to model the response for the students to hear and practise and might add words or phrases as necessary.

Substitution tables are provided to cover all stages of the process such as this example to support students in discussing, reading and writing about the specifications:

My game	will should must	be	bright and colourful easy to carry exciting to play

This allows the students to incorporate aesthetic and ergonomic considerations discovered during the investigations and makes them aware that these must feature in their own games. Once the students become familiar with the format and use of the substitution tables they can use them systematically to cover many of the features of the design brief. This has enabled the students to record difficult but necessary stages as ably as their more fluent peers. By using the tables, students learn and recognise recurrent vocabulary as well as synonyms, such as 'found', 'discovered' and 'learned'. Their attention can also be drawn to spelling and the phonic aspects of reading, such as syllabification.

When the students are ready they write up the first draft of their investigations, still in response to questions and using the substitution tables for support. They demonstrate their understanding through using the tables in relation to their own particular experiences and games, selecting the vocabulary that meets their needs. At this stage the sentences may be constructed as a list with no attempt to combine them into a cohesive piece, which comes later and involves using pronouns. This might help them understand the use of pronouns in cohesion, a feature that students often find difficult.

One student wrote a sample first paragraph;

> I investigated Snakes and Ladders. I found that Snakes and Ladders is a board game. I found that Snakes and Ladders is a counting game. I found that Snakes and Ladders looks colourful. I found that Snakes and Ladders looks attractive. I found that the base board has got a square shape. I found that the board is made of card. I found that the board is smooth. I found that Snakes and Ladders has got dice. I found that Snakes and Ladders has got pieces. I found that the pieces are made of plastic. I learned that the base board has got pictures on it. I learned that four people can play Snakes and Ladders. I learned that Snakes and Ladders is fun to play.

This was followed by a similar paragraph for each of the games she investigated. Each enabled her to practice forming meaning in English, initially by constructing simple sentences. At the second drafting stage attention was paid to cohesion, vocabulary extension and continuous paragraph writing with complex sentences where appropriate. I wrote a model paragraph and provided it as a reading activity and for students to use as a model for re-drafting their own writing.

> I investigated Snakes and Ladders. I found that **it** is a counting **and** board game. The board is made of card **which** is in a square shape. I **also** found that the board looks colourful **and** attractive **with** pictures on **it**. I learned that Snakes and Ladders has got pieces. **The** pieces are made of plain plastic **which** are in different colours. I **also** learned that four people can play **it and** that **it** is fun to play.

Access to the curriculum

Students need to be prepared for full access to the curriculum and this includes skills in formal English, using their mother tongues and peer support to help them progress. The current trend in literacy development is to use writing frames to scaffold students' development but these require the student to be able to read English and construct sentences needed by the frame. Early stage bilingual learners find this difficult because they lack the confidence to generate their own ideas and the vocabulary and sentence structure to express them. I chose to be more explicit about the learning and teaching process as it interfaces with learning English so that using a substitution table could become systematic and complement the technique of using a writing frame.

Design and Technology provides excellent contexts for language acquisition. Recurrent events invite repetition of language. The process of planning, creation, describing and recording findings takes place through a variety of complementary media, all of which can generate specific language structures for each of the elements. Students' expectations and experiences of the process can support prediction, a skill needed in reading. And it can also facilitate the students' ability to match symbols to actions. By making choices about tools, materials, shape and colour, students can give form to their creativity and express it by visual and linguistic means.

Substitution tables provide a firm basis for supporting reading and writing. Some students find acquiring English late in their schooling difficult, particularly if they are not literate in their first language. The development of writing skills is a slow, sometimes tedious process which takes a long period of continuous and regular practice. So clear targets must be set to ensure that the process is manageable, purposeful and relevant. Supporting early stage learners in interesting and challenging activities that take account of their prior knowledge, including mother tongue, is a way of maintaining motivation and development.

Initially the understanding and use of language is oral and aural, so throughout the Design project the students are encouraged to support their understanding with drawings, practical activities, using their mother tongues and discussion. When substitution tables are introduced, reading becomes necessary and students become acquainted with forms of English such as the sequence of words and sound and letter patterns in spelling.

Later attention to making a written record is mainly concerned with the skill of writing, once the concepts and ideas have been embedded. As a conscious and deliberate act the writing process can focus thinking when we deploy it to communicate meaning. Writing conventions, details of sound and spelling patterns can be demonstrated and students can see how the sentences in a paragraph relate to each other and the context. Those students who are at a stage of forming cohesive paragraphs are guided in doing so. Throughout the project the students are recording their observations and experiences and deriving meaning from text.

Extension activities enable students to practice using other aspects of language in their second and subsequent drafts. They have a context for using and understanding pronouns, subordinate clauses, phrases and connectives. In addition, words and phrases synonymous with those in the models can be introduced.

The format of DT recurs, ensuring that language students have practised and become familiar with is revisited and repeated in other projects. Much language learning is done informally without teacher intervention, by inductive thinking, observation and association. The skill lies in learning from how others use and model language. So the students' developing conceptual and critical understanding confirms their linguistic progress. With access to different forms of reading material and genuine communication they are exposed to the old models they have consciously learnt but also to new ones. The technique such as the writing frame, then, is a skill students can learn and then adapt to new language structures. And through repeated feedback and new experiences they can practise and reinforce the forms they have been exposed to and make them their own. As a consequence students develop intuitions about language use and begin to utilise them, secure in the knowledge of consciously acquired sentence structure through the use of substitution tables.

The recent political dimension to teaching

The lessons outlined in this chapter were taught by experienced language and curriculum development teachers working in partnership with subject specialists. They had been employed by the school in the early 1990s at the time of the high profile launch of the NFER partnership model of teaching (Bourne and McPake, 1991) and had, since then, been school based and school managed. In the new arrangements for EMTAG, managed by the DfEE, school management are looking towards a 'cheaper' future that will provide support to students through bilingual assistants, classroom assistants or main-scale teacher appointments rather than the quality provision that characterised partnership teaching. The partnership approach was often best illustrated in the work of skilled and trained – so comparatively 'expensive' – specialist teachers and the process of working partnerships enhanced the professional development of all the teachers involved.

Monitoring and responding to the differential between the achievement of students who are linguistically advantaged in English and bilingual students, and that between black and white monolingual students, is the challenge for the new Ethnic Minority and Traveller Achievement projects. The fact that these projects are lodged in schools should open a new era of institutional accountability for academically sound, antiracist provision. With ever finer tools for monitoring the achievement gaps, hard questions need to be faced such as how institutional racism affects the design of the curriculum and the criteria for educational success. Issues around the role of language in learning for all students remain vital. Responsibility for the process of language development for all students, including bilingual learners, in every discipline and by every teacher needs to be clearly understood and addressed at Initial Teacher Training level and featured in ongoing professional development.

Resources

Bygott, D (1992) *Black and British,* Oxford University Press

Frow, M (1996) *Roots of the Future*, Commission for Racial Equality

Rogers, J.A (1952) *Nature Knows No Colour Line*, Helga M.Rogers

Sancho, I (1997) *An African Man of Letters*, National Portrait Gallery

8

Developing language-aware teaching in secondary schools

Claire Edmunds

One student's experience

Twelve year old Mehmet and his mother are attending an interview in the school where he is shortly to become a student. Neither of them speaks English so an older student has been enlisted to interpret. Mehmet says that he enjoyed his primary school in Cyprus. His favourite subject was Maths. He is plainly excited at the prospect of starting school in Britain, but also daunted. His mother has one over-riding concern – that he should learn English. Much of the interview is devoted to discussing how this might be achieved. To her surprise, he will have a full timetable of mainstream subject lessons. A group of classmates have volunteered to look after him, both in lessons and during breaks. He is reassured that his English will develop quickly as he communicates with his new friends. They are looking forward to playing football with him. He is advised not to worry if he doesn't understand all that's going on in lessons – but to watch, listen and guess and to keep a record in Turkish – with some English if possible – of what he understands. He will be given a notebook to use as a bilingual diary. This can be a basis for talking to his mother about what he has been doing at school. It is appropriate that this discussion should be in Turkish, the language that he thinks in. He has the opportunity of becoming bilingual and biliterate and this will be a great advantage to him as he continues his studies. His ambition is to become a doctor. Mehmet seems reassured, his mother less so, but she is glad to hear confirmation of her own belief in the importance for him of maintaining and developing his home language.

Two years later Mehmet and his mother are attending a Year 9 parents' evening. An interpreter accompanies them but it is clear that Mehmet understands what each teacher has to say and is able to comment on his work. His Maths, History and French teachers have congratulated him on the progress he has made. He is in a top set for Maths and for French and his French teacher is keen to enter him for O level Turkish. His favourite subjects are Drama, History and Design Technology: he says they all include drawing, role-play and 'doing things' – he has enjoyed a recent History trip – and 'that make me understand'. But there are also severe disappointments. His report states that he 'lacks interest' in Science and has done no Geography homework. He admits to both teachers 'I not understand'. His tutor has noticed that he has had a few one day absences on a Thursday, the day the class have double Science.

Mehmet's experience is not untypical of bilingual beginners in secondary schools. If they have learnt Maths previously they are likely to engage quickly with Maths lessons in English: much of the symbolic system of computation is universal. Practical subjects can be relatively accessible because linguistic development is supported by practical understanding. Mehmet's success in History, a subject which relies heavily on text, is more surprising. However, where his experience does tally with that of most early-stage bilingual learners is the wide variation in his achievement, from success in some subjects to outright failure in others. This is often due less to subject differences than to the effect of different teaching strategies. Mehmet's experience in Science dramatically bears this out.

Mehmet is now at the end of Year 10. He is doing the full Science course and enjoying it. When his problems in Science were picked up, rather belatedly, in Year 9, it was decided to make this a priority. He was moved into a parallel Science group where the teacher was working in partnership with a colleague from the Language Development department (funded by EMTAG, the Ethnic Minority and Traveller Achievement Grant) to develop collaborative learning with an emphasis on hands-on activities, independent note-taking and discussion based on observation. Within a term Mehmet's work had improved dramatically.

Mehmet has renewed his ambition to study medicine, is working hard and feels he is doing well at school – or so he has written to his grandmother in Cyprus. He has passed O level Turkish with an A* and is expected to do as well in French. He dropped History on the advice of a new teacher who thought his essay style was not yet 'up to scratch'. His 'option' subjects are French, Art and Language Development, a non-examination study slot for bilingual learners, where they are given support in planning and redrafting course-work.

The importance of curriculum development supported by in-service training
Newly qualified teachers

Teaching is a complex skill, much of which develops through direct experience in the classroom. Pedagogies presented in college lectures, discussed in tutorials, identified in school observation sessions are not assimilated into practice until they have been personally tested in the classroom. This pragmatic process, begun during school teaching practice, should continue well into the first teaching post.

Newly qualified teachers, even those with special talent, need time and opportunity to apply and continually develop what they have learned during their training. How they approach this development work will depend upon four variables: their own social, political and educational perspectives, developed partly through personal experiences of learning; approaches recommended during their training and to which they feel drawn as being most in line with their personal views and experiences; approaches they have begun to adopt for themselves and found to be effective; and finally, approaches which have caught their attention while they observe other teachers' lessons.

The opportunity to observe a range of classroom teaching and learning is particularly effective in laying foundations for good teaching – teaching which facilitates learning for the whole class. Watching and reflecting upon children as they respond differently to a variety of methodologies can provide crucial insights into two basic issues: the use of class-teaching strategies which can stimulate and support learning for all the students in a class of varied abilities and cultural or linguistic backgrounds; and in-built differentiation which empowers individual students and ensures their full participation by building upon their particular prior knowledge and experience and their personal learning strategies.

Resolving these fundamental issues is a matter for each individual teacher, each group of colleagues, each school. What is important is the process of developing insights and related practical expertise; and for all teachers, whatever their length of experience, this can only be achieved by maintaining an alert, reflective and empirical view of classroom successes and failures and being ready to respond by making changes to both curriculum content and style of delivery.

Enjoying, or at least surviving, the first year in post may depend largely on influences not directly related to quality of teaching. Other determining factors will include: students' prior experiences and expectations of learning and being taught, established class-room dynamics, as well as the teacher's charisma and social skills, her commitment, confidence – and sheer stamina. Ultimately, how-ever, pedagogy will become the most important factor. In the long term, only good teaching can ensure successful learning and maxi-mum achievement for the students.

What is meant by 'good' or 'effective' teaching – the 'good practice' extolled by educationists and by teachers themselves – varies from individual to individual, from school to school and has long been a political football. For the purpose of this chapter it should be interpreted as teaching which promotes equality of opportunity to learn confidently and reach individual potential through academic achievement.

Continuing professional development for all teachers

The development of good practice depends largely on teachers' con-tinuing readiness to adopt a reflective, experiential approach to their work. Perhaps the most exciting aspect of teaching is the oppor-tunity to learn through doing it: the opportunity constantly to develop and refine one's practice by observing and monitoring students' learning, and using this information to evaluate teaching strategies – a pattern of low-key but continuous personal action research.

However, this development work can only be effective if it is under-pinned by sound principles; by an understanding of basic educa-tional concepts and how to apply them systematically to classroom practice through a range of strategies. And theory itself is develop-mental. Current educational research and debate can continuously trigger new insights, new perspectives, as they resonate with personal classroom experience.

For this thinking to have any practical impact on their work, busy teachers need not only time to read but also regular opportunity to reflect, talk through ideas with colleagues and collaborate with them to develop any relevant adaptations to curriculum content or delivery. Personal professional development does not happen in isolation. It relies upon regular discussion and sharing of good practice.

Similarly, at the institutional level, effective and sustained development depends upon much more than individual initiatives in isolated classrooms. It requires structured, collaborative development systems, underpinned by whole-school policy and ongoing management support, in order to disseminate and extend improving practice throughout the school. Students need consistent routines and systematic consolidation of their developing knowledge and learning skills. Effective teaching and learning depend upon this principle of sustained development and consolidation. In secondary schools, where teaching is divided between distinct subject areas and responsibility for each student's learning is shared by several teachers from different academic disciplines, it is particularly important that teachers work and plan together to ensure consistent development of good practice across the curriculum.

A useful model of cross-curricular planning is to be seen in many primary schools, with their one-class one-teacher organisation. Indeed it will be clear that some of the teaching strategies recommended in this chapter – such as integrated oracy and literacy development, flexible group work and the encouragement of independent research – are common primary practice and familiar to Year 7 children starting in their new secondary school. It has become increasingly common for Year 6 and Year 7 teachers to visit each other's classrooms and discuss how their relative pedagogies can be more closely linked. Where this has been done successfully, Year 7 classrooms have seemed much less daunting to the new arrivals and their confidence as learners better sustained. And the secondary teachers have gained useful insights from primary practice with its greater emphasis on language development.

The school in-service programme

Theoretical input on Initial Teacher Training courses has been largely replaced by longer stints of practical experience in schools, supported by on-site tutorials by college tutors and school mentors and followed in the induction year by a regular programme of in-service training. 'Directed time' in schools, though initially resisted for being autocratically imposed, has brought the possibility of regular professional development for the whole staff. This has given all teachers, including the most experienced, opportunities to update their thinking and practice.

A cohesive, structured in-service programme that is linked to on-going curriculum development and supported by collaborative planning, trialing, monitoring, evaluation and dissemination to colleagues, will be welcomed as both relevant and effective. The in-service education should balance theory and practical application and will be even more popular if there is some flexibility and choice: e.g. rolling programmes timed to fit in with individual timetables. This approach has stimulated new departmental or inter-departmental curriculum development initiatives, piloted by self-selected teachers whose enthusiasm can be infectious.

A well-planned and democratically agreed school in-service programme, linked to induction for newly qualified staff and closely integrated with ongoing curriculum development projects, can engender a whole-school ethos of reflective teaching. Within such an ethos the individual practitioner is supported by continuing discussion and practical collaboration with colleagues and whole-staff and subject-department meetings will give priority to curriculum development issues, with discussion constantly translated into practical outcomes.

Two key principles of learning: relevance and the role of language

Advances in teaching methodology over the last thirty years have come from new understandings in two areas; the relevance to students of what is taught and the role of language in learning. A clear understanding of these important principles should inform and direct all curriculum development and have priority in school in-service programmes.

Relevance

The influence of child psychology and the resulting learner-oriented view of education has led to a school curriculum better tailored in all subjects to children's interests and personal experience. The choice of set literary texts has moved from monocultural, anglo-centric classics to a multicultural selection of texts which feature child characters and situations closer to the life experience of the students. In Science, theory is regularly related to everyday situations – cooking, riding a bike. GCSE coursework is open to choice, with students opting for RE projects on their own religion; Technology projects suit their taste in fashion or leisure pursuits; their local area can be the focus of geographical or sociological studies. The use of IT opens up a world of personally-selected research topics.

The role of language

Understanding the central role of language in learning, as articulated by the Russian psychologist, Vygotsky, and developed by educationists such as Krashen and Cummins, has been slow to take root and affect practice, particularly in secondary and higher education. In primary schools, with their responsibility for initial literacy, issues of language have traditionally been more to the fore. Primary teachers have long been familiar with the concept and practical implications of language development, encouraging children to express their ideas and experiences both orally – through the daily routine of personal news telling, for example – and in reading and writing. Children are urged to read newspaper reports and 'information books' as well as 'stories' and to extend their use of genres and vocabulary – to 'use longer words' and to write letters, reports, plays, poems.

In secondary schools, recognition of language development as an integral part of content learning has been more patchy. This may be due partly to greater curriculum fragmentation and subject specialism; partly to the overloaded content of many areas of the National Curriculum; and partly to a traditional presumption among secondary teachers – as well as parents and the students themselves – that literacy teaching is the responsibility of the primary school. It is still commonly argued that once children are literate, more advanced subject teaching can follow smoothly, and the development of language skills can be confined to the English and Modern Foreign Language curriculums.

Despite difficulties and restrictions, there have been pockets of real advance in some primary and secondary schools, LEAs and regions. These have arisen almost exclusively in response to the particular needs of bilingual learners – students from a variety of cultures and whose home language is not English. From this work have emerged important new insights into the learning process itself, with implications for a relevant multicultural curriculum and, more radically, a pedagogy which clearly recognises the crucial role of language in all learning, in terms of both curriculum access and personal language development.

Where these insights have informed practice, the result has been not only improved access to the mainstream curriculum for bilingual learners but also increased confidence and higher achievement for all students, as the academic language of the curriculum becomes more accessible to them and forms a more coherent part of their working repertoire.

Implementing change: teacher input and student learning activities

Attention to the two key conditions of learning mentioned above – relevance of content and a full role for language – has generated fundamental changes in pedagogy, which have entailed some careful rethinking of entrenched approaches. It is important that this process continues and extends to all schools and across all subject areas.

When incorporating such new thinking into their regular planning and development work, whether sketching individual lesson plans or adjusting current schemes of work and devising new ones, teachers may find it useful to address separately two closely related areas of the work – teacher input and student learning activities – to look critically at both and ensure that each supports the other.

Teacher input would concentrate on making the curriculum accessible to students. Teachers do this partly through content – optimising its relevance to students' prior experience and existing understandings, by careful selection of the examples, hypotheses and opinions used to illustrate the key facts and concepts to be taught – and partly through their style of presentation. In addition they would develop strategies to improve students' access skills, by promoting active listening and reading.

Regarding learning activities, teachers would aim to motivate and enable students to rehearse, internalise and make their own what they have heard and read. To this end they focus on student-student and student-teacher interaction for collaborative learning. The tasks set aim to develop students' oral and literacy skills. This means extending the linguistic repertoire to include academic genres and vocabulary and developing students' critical language skills through active listening, discussion and focused, reflective reading and writing. Students would be encouraged to express opinions and review and assess their own work.

In both areas – teacher input or student activities – the overall aim is to empower students to take charge of their own learning through confident use of language. Talk is paramount – interactive teaching, encouraging questions and discussion, and collaborative tasks. Both aspects emphasise the use of talk to model and develop the subject-specific written language required for academic success and to develop thinking.

Outlined below are practical strategies for implementing these changes. All are relevant for all students, but aspects of particular relevance for bilingual students are indicated in italics.

Accessible teacher input: relevance
Making links with prior experience and understandings in the multicultural classroom

Teacher talk and the language of textbooks must be capable of holding students' attention. For this, it must first be accessible. The cry of 'it's boring!' is often a synonym for 'I don't understand.'

A teacher's first response to this could be, 'you must learn to listen' or 'you need to improve your reading'. However, the problem may well lie deeper. It may be that the content itself is inaccessible because it fails to link in any meaningful way with students' personal experiences and interpretations of the world around them. All new information, if it is to be understood, must relate in some way to established understandings, to the individual learner's internal model of reality. This important principle of learning has been explored by many educationists. In Frank Smith's words, 'if the situation confronting us cannot be related to our theory of the world, then there can be no comprehension and no learning' (Smith, 1978)

Using students' out-of-school understandings

Teachers regularly illustrate difficult or unfamiliar concepts by providing commonly experienced, day-to-day examples. They relate laboratory chemical reactions to kitchen incidents or bias in historical sources to the reporting of a football match by a team supporter. In many classrooms this practice has been adapted to suit the increasing cultural diversity of the students. Most teachers are now aware that experiences which are commonplace for some may be unknown to others, whether it be Saturday night discos, caravan weekends, bilingual family discussion or specific religious celebrations. In the inner city some students may have little experience of the countryside while others may have travelled the world and spent their childhood in rural India or Somalia. Integrating references to these various experiences into classroom learning has been a mainstay of the multicultural curriculum. Many classrooms have become places where these experiences can be shared, widening horizons and creating new understandings, to the benefit of all the students.

A monocultural curriculum, unadapted to the different experiences, perspectives and expectations of the students from ethnic minority groups, can seriously impede those students' learning and deny their right of access to the curriculum. By contrast, incorporating and building upon these experiences and perspectives helps to explain things which would otherwise be difficult to understand and makes them more compelling. Bilingual students also have a role as contributors to class learning – both in their own eyes and in the eyes of the rest of the class. This social and academic inclusion is an important pre-condition for learning.

An effective context for inclusion for bilingual learners is Language Awareness. An incident witnessed in a London School in the 1970s provides a dramatic example. A Vietnamese student, recently arrived from a refugee camp in Hong Kong and understanding little English, had found little acceptance among his classmates and was being subjected to constant out-of-class bullying by some of them. The aim of one lesson was to give students an experience of various scripts, including Vietnamese. The new arrival was asked to demonstrate on the board and the teacher advised students who wished to try writing the letters themselves to consult him. Suddenly he became a classroom consultant, an expert. The bullying ceased from that day.

Creating shared understandings in the classroom

Whilst personal background experience is important, learning experiences are also created and developed in the classroom itself. Any shared classroom stimulus – a picture, text, practical experiment or creative activity – responded to jointly through collaborative tasks and discussion, can provide a valuable shared reference point on which to build further understandings.

In one school a Year 7 English scheme of work entitled 'Inventions' began with two complicated, unconventional drawings: a Heath Robinson illustration of an anti-litter machine and a teacher's Heath Robinson-inspired drawing of postman's bike, complete with letter rack, heated handle bars, snack bar and 'fierce dog repellent'. Discussion about interpreting the drawings led to a shared understanding of invention as a useful response to practical problems that involved creativity and fantasy. Follow-on tasks included creative writing about students' own inventions, and exercises in persuasion and marketing. This led finally to discussion that linked literature and creative writing with Technology coursework and Science and Mathematics investigations and showed collaborative understanding of the concepts of imagination, inventiveness, invention and research.

Understanding what counts as achievement

Shared classroom experience also involves understanding of another kind – emerging perceptions about procedures and expectations – the very process of teaching and learning in that particular school of that particular subject area.

Students who have experienced a more formal style of teaching and have no experience of creative writing may find the fanciful presentation of the concept of invention and the 'mad inventor' task puzzling and irrelevant. The concept of 'invention' might be unclear to them and will not help them engage with the notion of process as an end in itself, in the context of Technology, Maths or Science.

Equally, in Science lessons, bilingual students may focus on getting the tasks 'right', even if this means imitating what others are doing, rather than working out a problem. So they might not have internalised the task and it will not have the same significance for them as a shared reference point. These are the students who might be confused by the request to 'show your working out' for Maths or to describe mistakes and rethinking in a Technology design project.

To ensure that both *what* is taught and *how* relates to the learner's established understandings, teachers must first know something about students' prior school experience as well as their family background.

For students whose previous formal education has taken place in another country their prior knowledge and, even more importantly, their understanding through experience of the process and expectations of formal school learning may differ fundamentally from that of their classmates. It is not easy for individual teachers to acquire all such information without a school system which ensures full and relevant records based upon dialogue with students and their families. And without this information it is all too easy to make false assumptions about students' learning needs.

Interaction as a tool for assessing prior understanding

Even in a stable and culturally homogenous group, or one where differences in cultural and educational experience are understood and taken into account in order to help individuals develop understanding of the curriculum, the mental models generated in any lesson will vary considerably and be difficult for the teacher to gauge. An accurate idea of what has been understood can only come from the students themselves as they express their developing understanding. Some evidence may be found in students' written work where their personal perspectives may be glimpsed through the opinions or judgements they offer. But a clear picture is more likely to emerge through talk, with a teacher or peer asking them to expand or explain ideas. How they do this can shed light on the extent of their understanding, as well as providing a valuable on-the-spot teaching opportunity.

In the following example the Science teacher is able to recognise and put right a seeming misconception – that electric current involves both positive and negative charges. He also models 'electrons' as a replacement for 'things'

Student A: (*reading from the board*) What does a Van de Graaff generator do?

Student B: It charges you up . .

Student A: Yes – makes you electric – with . . little . . um . . things . . and they jump across and go into you

Teacher: Electrons

Student A: Yes

Student B: And they're positive and negative

Student A: Yes

Teacher: Positive *and* negative electrons! Now which are they?

Student A: Just . . negative?

Teacher: Yes! Remember! There *are* two types of charges . .

Student B: (*interrupting*) . . positive and negative!

Teacher: But which sort of charges move?

Student A: Negative charges

Teacher: Yes – and they're the ones called .

Student A: Electrons.

Teacher: So an electric current is actually . .

Both students: Electrons

Teacher: (gesture)

Both students: ... moving!

'Brainstorming'

Using talk to extract and build on students' knowledge by brain-storming is a well established strategy in secondary classrooms. This simple method of passing the initiative from teacher to learners ensures that the ensuing lesson is supported by the students' prior knowledge. As they explain and discuss their knowledge, the basic learning process – that of students focusing on their personal understandings, making them explicit and then adapting them to accommodate new ones – is facilitated.

An initial brainstorm could lead into a prioritising/categorising exercise to encourage further analysis, thereby matching personal knowledge to the curriculum learning to follow. Regular blackboard modelling of brainstorming and subsequent concept mapping encourages students to use these strategies for themselves, either during group activities or for individual work.

Bilingual learners whose English is not fluent may find it daunting to voice an opinion publicly. For them small group brainstorming is an important means of access, particularly if sensitively supported by the teacher. Students who have received formal education outside the UK may be unfamiliar with this use of personal experience for learning and will need encouragement and practice. A brainstorming exercise should be approached after discussion in the student's first language with a peer, teacher or classroom assistant. The discovery that their own personal knowledge has a place in formal learning is encouraging and motivating for all learners. For bilingual learners it can be a watershed, particularly if the subject is one about which they feel they are expert, e.g. the experience and process of language acquisition discussed in a Language Awareness session.

Accessible teacher input: language and additional cues to meaning
The process of learning and language development

Learning and language development form one indivisible process, made up of developing understanding of new concepts and, simultaneously, of the language through which they are expressed. The process involves accessing and so acquiring language as its meaning is guessed at and, at least partially, revealed, 'getting the gist' by actively making sense of text; of focusing first on content and thence assimilating the form of its expression. And, in conjunction with all this, it involves the process of developing language by using it – listening, speaking, reading and writing – and gradually developing and consolidating meanings through repeated use of words and phrases in different contexts, until they are established as personal repertoire. This complex process is similar for all learners, whether infants learning to speak their mother tongue or older learners developing new language skills. It applies to all students, whether bilingual and learning through the medium of a whole new additional language or whether native English speakers acquiring new academic vocabulary and genres in their first language.

Accessible language

For text to be meaningful, not every word need be familiar. All that listeners or readers require to give them access to text are sufficient cues to make some sense of it and to be interested in making more. These cues emanate partly from contextual links with the learners' own knowledge and understanding (see 'Relevance' above) and partly from the language itself – its structure and cohesion (see Introduction), its conceptual flow. So teacher explanations and information texts need to be precisely worded and well thought through.

Not that students should be fed a diet of simplified text. Summaries and paragraph headings are useful as pointers to conceptual structure and as *aides-memoires* but all students should be given the opportunity to engage with sustained discussion and to read a range of complete, detailed texts.

In the passage that introduces the alimentary canal (see 'Contextualisation' below) the students are immediately confronted with a lengthy passage of quite difficult text. The sequencing task they are given, requiring them to scan the text with a clear, limited focus, enables them to read purposefully and without undue difficulty.

In an English lesson, a first reading of *Macbeth* Act 1 Scene iii, supported by a taped recording, is followed closely and with sustained interest by all the students, regardless of their reading ability. This would not be possible without preparatory work which has created a mental picture of the setting – a wind-swept heath – explored the concepts of superstition and ambition by relating them to the students' own experience, given an outline of the situation and used images and creative role-play to bring meaning and familiarity to a few selected quotations which are now recognisable in context. Important additional cues come from the actors' expressive reading, which emphasises the drama and poetic rhythm of the words.

In a Personal and Social Education class, the topic is bullying and its link with racism. A lively discussion is sustained for the full half hour and is closely followed by all the students, including two whose command of English probably affords only partial understanding of what is said and whose contributions are monosyllabic. But for them the subject clearly resonates with their own experience.

Bilingual learners need full immersion in the language of the curriculum if they are eventually to acquire the full repertoire of English vocabulary and genres they will need for academic success. It is important too that the content of the language they meet in lessons reflects their own conceptual level (see 'Interaction' below). Access to text comes largely from non-linguistic contextual cues.

The introduction of new concepts or new areas of the curriculum can entail a host of new vocabulary and sometimes a completely new genre. Planning is required. Not only should the new concepts be linked to students' prior knowledge, but the language itself should be defined and associated with other contexts: in Science the flow of electrons can be compared to the flow of a river, attraction between electrons and protons associated with the familiar concept 'opposites attract'. New, abstract terminology needs to be defined in familiar, concrete language: 'substance' defined as 'the stuff something is made of', an insulator described as 'a substance which does not allow electricity to flow through it'.

Then, once introduced, it is important that the new terms – and the new genre in which they sit – continue to be used in an increasing range of contexts, both in class and for homework, until consolidated as part of students' established repertoire.

Older bilingual learners who are already familiar with abstract terminology in their first language need to be given access wherever possible through the short cut of translation by a bilingual teacher or through a bilingual dictionary or wall chart.

Visual cues

Probably the best known and most effective strategy for accessing difficult text is through illustration. An abstruse academic lecture can be clarified and made stimulating by appropriate slides. Television documentaries, which rely on pictorial images, have brought new knowledge to a wide and largely inexpert audience. Printed text can be made much more accessible by relevant illustrations.

Pictures, photographs, video, diagrams, charts, tables etc. make both teacher talk and textbooks clearer and more interesting. Explanations are better understood if supported by meaningful facial expression and gestures and written text is made more accessible by layout: headings, subheadings, paragraphs, font change to indicate emphasis or differentiation, boxing to draw attention to examples, instructions or summaries and so on.

The effect of all these non-linguistic visual cues is to consolidate the meanings of the text through an additional medium, lending added interest and appeal and giving extra information about for example, physical context, colour, shape, spatial relationships, emotional atmosphere and personality. The personality of fictitious characters in a set text can be given new depth by drawings or a video. In Geography unfamiliar landscapes or urban developments are best introduced by photographs.

For many bilingual learners visual cues provide an invaluable non-linguistic route to meaning, a bridge between guessing and understanding. For beginners in English, explanations based on pictures or charts are a prime means of access to the curriculum and if these students are not literate in their home language, visual cues may initially provide their only access into text.

For visual cues to be effective in clarifying text, they must be clearly linked to it, both visually and linguistically. Pictures and diagrams are most effective if labelled or captioned with words taken from the text and have less impact if the text they refer to is on another page. Teachers should support a class presentation or discussion by writing key points on the board. Sketches, symbols and diagrams, key words and headings will support students' understanding while also providing a record and *aide-memoire*.

Concrete examples

Visuals have another important function. They help students understand abstract concepts by linking them to concrete examples. A written definition of kinetic energy becomes clearer when illustrated by a bird in flight. One student illustrated the relationship between positive and negative electrons with a sketch of a child hand in hand with a large robot and captioned it 'opposites attract'. Abstractions, as their name implies, derive from concrete experience. A practical demonstration or picture alongside the text can initiate or reinforce a concept. The link between theory and example needs to be clearly understood and recognisable and must connect with students' experiences. If an example is misunderstood the result will be confusion.

For bilingual learners the concrete contextualisation of abstract concepts is particularly important. Acquiring a first or additional language begins with the concrete language of practical experience and the physical world, with its wealth of visual, non-linguistic cues to meaning. More complex, abstract understandings and the language to express them develop later. Even older students who are experienced in understanding and manipulating abstract concepts in their first language begin with concrete expressions in a new language, although translation can help to accelerate this process. The language of scientific theory will be learnt in the practical Science lesson, where spoken and written scientific language is used, modelled, clearly embedded in practical demonstration and explanatory visuals. As for all students, it must also be linked to familiar practical applications but these need careful selection: a thatched roof, a weather vane, roller skates may have little resonance with a student recently arrived from Somalia.

'Key visuals'

Illustrations can also be used to represent abstract structures directly. Concepts and the relationships between them can be shown in diagrammatic form: e.g. a flow diagram demonstrating the rain cycle or a graph plotting a relationship between rainfall and altitude. These 'graphic organisers' or 'key visuals' are powerful teaching tools. When planning to introduce an abstract concept it is advisable to support it with a key visual. Plans, diagrams, graphs etc can be used to present a succinct and easily accessible summary of the ideas presented in a lesson or a picture might serve this purpose. The concept of invention was neatly conveyed by the Heath Robinson drawing of a litter machine, which encapsulated notions of creative response to a need.

Key visuals can support teacher presentations and help to direct and structure students' understanding. They can then be used as scaffolding for the students' responses, whether orally or in writing, and as a basis for review or recap at the end of a lesson, consolidating and clarifying understandings. And they can provide a useful *aide-memoire* for revision purposes.

To bilingual learners these key visuals, with their potential to express complex meanings without recourse to language, are keys to understanding text and scaffolding for creating their own oral or written explanations (see 'Facilitated speaking' below).

Linking spoken and written language

Spoken and written language are mutually supportive. Text which is both seen and read aloud is strongly reinforced, be it textbook instructions or a passage of poetry. Key technical vocabulary and turns of phrase from subject textbooks written in subject-specific academic language should regularly be read aloud by the teacher so that the words become common currency as the students discuss and record their work.

This double impact of the spoken and written language is highly supportive for students for whom English is not well established. For beginners in English who are literate in their first language the literacy is transferable between languages. These students often find written English more accessible than the spoken form and relating talk to the written form is helpful.

For students who are not literate in their first language English can only be acquired through its spoken form. Their early literacy development can be greatly supported if the written form is immediately related to its sound e.g. group reading or listening to taped stories while following the printed text.

Matching teaching and learning styles
Contextualisation

Contextual cues are a significant means of acquiring new language and new understandings and of especial help to bilingual students developing the academic concepts and language of the curriculum. We have seen that contextual cues include references to prior knowledge and also concrete referents and visual illustration.

Teaching activities can also be planned to model the learning process. Take the example of a Year 10 Science class being re-introduced to the digestive system. Most students were taught about it in Year 8 but it may be new to others. When planning the scheme of work, the teacher selected activities which closely reflect the purpose of the learning: for students to understand the digestive system as a sequential, functional process and to describe it in terms of the names, physical characteristics and physical and chemical functions of each of the organs. The activities are developmental – increasingly difficult, both conceptually and in terms of language demands – and aim to reinforce the linguistic and conceptual process of students' own learning. The stages of this dual learning process are as follows:

1. An initial brainstorm establishes that most students understand the overall function of digestion, though they largely express it in non-scientific language. 'Food gives you energy so that you can stay alive – it has to be changed to get the good bits out – waste comes out again'. This process involves 'teeth, saliva and stomach'. 'Food is made up of different nutrients; carbohydrates – that's starch and sugar, protein and fat'. This has been taught recently in Food Technology. A student suggests that 'nutrients' is the scientific word for 'good bits'. More alternative words are supplied by individual students – 'digested', 'excreted', 'anus'. It is agreed that what they now need to find out is exactly how food is changed through digestion and where the nutrients 'land up'. 'They might go into your heart'.

The brainstorming task reflects the first stage in the learning process: identifying prior knowledge and also knowledge gaps, in order to predict a purpose for the new topic and to establish existing understandings. The language involved is exploratory group discussion, facilitated by the teacher, drawing attention to some new technical terms, both orally and in writing. Through this discussion a basic concept is introduced: of digestion as a functional process involving change.

2. Students are divided into groups of four and each group given some cards. On each card is printed the name of a digestive organ and a description of its function. Students share out the cards and work in pairs to scan them for words which suggest what happens to food as it is digested. Words suggested include 'churned', 'mixed' and 'broken down'.

This activity involves reading – scanning text for specific words or phrases with a specified meaning. The reading is scaffolded. It has a clear, limited purpose and is further supported by collaboration. It consolidates and develops the concept of digestion as a functional process involving change, by focusing on familiar words which suggest physical change to the students.

3. Words selected by the groups are pooled and the teacher writes them on the board, grouping together those referring to a physical process ('chewed', 'churned up', 'mixed', 'pass through', 'absorbed', 'squirted out', 'stored', 'egested') and those referring to a chemical process ('broken down into smaller particles', 'emulsifies', 'goes

acid', 'neutralises'). The class discusses how the two groups of words differ. During the discussion the words 'chemical change' and 'enzyme' are written on the board and defined.

All this involves three simple language tasks:

- listening to other students reading out single words and phrases

- selecting and reading out other words from the group lists

- scanning the text on the board in order to understand the teacher's categorisation.

Conceptually, this activity aims to help students understand a specific aspect of the digestive process – the distinction between physical and chemical change.

4. The next task requires students in their groups to sequence the cards and identify the links between them. At first this seems easy. The mouth obviously comes first and the repeat of 'bolus' puts the oesophagus second; 'waste' and 'anus' put the large intestine last. Positioning the duodenum, stomach and small intestine is more difficult. Two of the organs seem to share a function. The two cards concerned are searched more closely for sequential clues:

> 'I'm confused – that says 'proteins are broken down' and there it is again 'proteins are broken down'

> 'Look there – it says 'the digestion of proteins is begun' – so that comes first'

> 'But there it says 'digestion is continued''

> 'No, that's for starch. That starts in the mouth'

> 'Here – 'acid produced in the stomach is neutralised' – so that does come after stomach'

> 'Here's another – 'finally absorbed into the bloodstream''

The teacher circulates among the groups, confirms the sequence of organs and encourages students to make a note of the textual evidence they used.

This activity, like the second, involves scaffolded reading. The task of sequencing gives a clear purpose and scanning the text for clues is supported by exploratory discussion. But closer, more thoughtful reading is required because the pattern of sequential clues is complex. This task develops the students' understanding of digestion by introducing the concept of a unifying sequential pattern which brings together a multiplicity of physical and chemical processes.

5. For the plenary feedback the teacher produces a large coloured chart showing the digestive tract. A volunteer labels the individual organs, confirming the sequence agreed by all the groups. Volunteers from each group are now invited in turn to quote and explain the textual clues that helped in the sequencing task.

With the diagram as a focus, there follows an informal quiz, with groups taking turns to field questions. One student remains in front and points to the relevant part of the diagram as the discussion progresses. The teacher intervenes only when necessary, to rectify a misconception or pursue a useful avenue of questioning. She also selects the participants to ensure fair distribution. The first questioner wants to know 'how it doesn't get stuck.' Further questions, suggestions and answers lead to a negotiated explanation of the role of muscle movement, chemical break-down and absorption. New vocabulary and word-use are explained by the teacher; key words such as 'contract', 'wall', 'blood stream', and some definitions are written on the board. Finally, a student volunteers to summarise the digestive process. He uses terms such as 'liquidising', 'separating out insoluble bits', 'chemical breaking down' and 'absorption into the blood stream'.

This task involves prolonged discussion with some sustained explanation of complex processes. More formal scientific language is used, reflecting the academic genre of the text. Using the diagram helps to structure the questioning – for example, holding attention on one particular organ or on a sequence of changes along the digestive tract.

Conceptually this activity involves the development of a holistic understanding of the digestive system, as one coherent sequential pattern. The diagram supports this comprehensive understanding.

6. The sixth task is to construct a detailed written grid to show not only the sequence of organs but also the distinctive digestive process for each type of nutrient, linking each enzyme to each chemical change. The agreed sequence of organs is written in first, the name of each read aloud by the students in turn and the spelling checked. Individuals or pairs then take responsibility for tracking the sequence of chemical changes for each nutrient. The results are shared by

dictating them to the group. One group decides to colour-code the progress of each nutrient. The rest of the grid is completed in pairs.

Completing the grid involves collaborative, scaffolded writing in note form, for which the grid provides a detailed structure. The writing is supported by discussion and by a third reading of the text to decide on the correct wording and spelling.

Conceptually, this restructuring task involves a re-analysis of the digestive system with separate processes clearly and separately detailed and located within the overall process.

7. The homework is to write a description of the digestion of boiled rice, grilled fish or ice cream. Each group arranges to cover all three between them, as the work is to be used for a group presentation next lesson.

In terms of language, the task includes reading research to check the dietary components of the chosen food, followed by sustained independent writing in an appropriate academic genre.

Conceptually, this involves understanding the dietary components of different foodstuffs and analysing the digestive system to select the parts relevant to one particular application.

Interaction

Most of the tasks described above involve talk among the students as they develop ideas and make decisions about what they have to do and how best to do it. Some of this discussion also involves the teacher who circulates among the groups to facilitate the learning, asking and responding to questions. Students come to understand the purpose of the task as they take turns, watch and listen to each other and become actively involved. They negotiate meaning for themselves as they indicate what puzzles them and where they need support or where they can add their own comments and additional insights. They constantly seek, often successfully, to link their own ideas with the language of the reference book or worksheet, as they work together and compare notes, searching through text, consulting diagrams, making notes, constantly discussing their findings and what to do next.

This collaboration works well with mixed-ability groups. More able students have opportunities to explain and elucidate for others – a challenging route to enhancing their own understanding – and others are well supported.

The teacher is the facilitator: organising and explaining the activities, then quietly circulating, responding to questions by giving extra clues rather than a full answer, further empowering the students as they guide their own learning.

Interactive talk should feature throughout a lesson, even when the teacher is addressing the whole class. The result is then a unified, lively classroom culture which empowers all students, whatever their National Curriculum level or immediate language ability.

Where interaction is routine and well structured, it is easy for bilingual students to understand the rules and become more closely involved in the learning. Teacher explanations which take the form of dialogue provide a model for group discussion. Having heard other students comment and ask questions, it seems less daunting for bilingual learners to ask for help themselves when they lose the thread – at least in the context of a small group. The language continues to be clearly linked to the task. The discussion is repetitive and developmental as different students repeat and develop findings for themselves. It is relatively easy for unconfident learners to feel part of this group as they seek for ideas rather than simply reiterate or copy words with apparent acceptance and understanding.

Bilingual learners need to be in mixed-ability groups which provide good language models and help them to operate at the intellectual level at which they operate in their first language.

Collaborative group work also enables teachers to support bilingual learners. They can facilitate group co-operation and draw in unconfident students. They can differentiate their response to individual students, taking opportunities to model academic language, using repetition and asking questions which use the words of the required response without giving away the answer.

Student empowerment

The pedagogy described in this chapter empowers the learners. It is fired by an understanding that both the ideas and the language taught are to be grasped by students and made their own. This process of assimilation is begun as they recognise the relevance to their own experience of what is taught and so make place for it within their conceptual maps. The process continues as the language of these new ideas is used and finally owned by them to be used spontaneously as part of their personal repertoire. The key to this process of developing ownership lies in interactional language and learning, modelled by a style of teaching which maintains dialogue with students.

Facilitating students' language development: classroom strategies
A holistic, cross-curricular approach

Pilot schemes to introduce the National Literacy Strategy into secondary schools, with their separate subject areas, again highlights the importance of a cross-curricular language policy. This ensures that literacy is properly located as a fully integrated part of all subject teaching and empowers students to develop their language in context through listening, speaking, reading and writing in interaction with both teachers and peers.

The four language skills are interlinked and should be developed together in mutually supportive combinations, for example: collaborative reading activities with text read aloud and discussed; collaborative redrafting of written work – 'conferencing'; oral presentation of printed text or written work; written recording of spoken language, as for questionnaires.

To develop such a balanced, holistic approach to language, teachers need to examine the learning process separately for each language skill and consider how best to support it through appropriate teaching strategies in their particular subject.

The receptive skills: listening and reading

Although they are defined as receptive skills to distinguish them from the productive skills of speaking and writing, listening and reading for learning are not passive. Both depend on having a purpose and a clear focus. Purposeful, selective listening and reading empower and motivate students and give them access to language which they might otherwise dismiss as 'too difficult'.

'Why can't you listen?' Being expected to listen quietly and passively to teacher talk is a common cause of classroom boredom. In order to listen attentively, students need to be actively involved with what is being said. So teachers need an interactive style which empowers the students by inviting comment and questions.

Students also need a clear purpose and focus for listening. 'Several of the people in this scene have prejudiced views. Listen to see if you can pick them out' is more likely to command attention than 'Listen carefully to this'. Explanations supported by a visual structure – blackboard headings and key points or related pictures or diagrams – can further focus listening and so give better access to new ideas and unfamiliar language.

Structured group discussion is particularly effective. When taking turns to report findings students often listen attentively to one another and teachers can intervene to clarify or extend ideas. These informal teacher-student dialogues, whether with groups, pairs or individuals, also provide opportunities for students to hear new academic language in context. The confidence, skill and close listening which students acquire through structured group discussion will be of benefit in GCSE English oral tasks

Facilitated reading

Reading too requires focus, otherwise texts can appear boring, difficult and inaccessible. Students access a story through the narrative – focusing on what will happen next. Reading for information requires a focus on the specific information, whether through scanning a text to identify the function of the digestive organs or to determine the characteristics of a historic person or setting.

The process of reading is a dialogue between reader and text, with reader acting as interrogator. This process is facilitated through Directed Activities Related to Text (DARTs) exercises (see Lunzer and Gardner,1984). When marking or manipulating text in the context of a structured activity with a clearly-defined, limited purpose, students are led into a systematic focus on meaning. They can transfer this approach to all their reading and gain the confidence to attempt more complex texts.

DARTs activities include: marking text to indicate specific information; sequencing text which has been jumbled; matching exercises – e.g. matching captions to pictures, phrases to definitions, abstract concepts to examples. Particular exercises can relate to particular curriculum demands. Sequencing is useful when teaching processes such as the steps taken in a scientific experiment. Matching exercises can help to define abstract concepts: matching 'simile' or 'metaphor' to concrete examples; matching examples of cause and effect to help understand causal relationship. Gap-filling can consolidate students' understanding of new academic terminology. Students who are given a way into text through techniques such as these develop the confidence to tackle seemingly difficult text. Enhanced confidence motivates them to greater interaction with text and increases the range of language they can access.

It is vital to ensure that bilingual learners with limited understanding of English are given a focus and purpose for accessing English text – spoken or written. Merely 'getting the gist', although useful for acquiring language, is unlikely to help them fulfil the requirements of a specific learning task.

The productive skills: speaking and writing

The scholastic achievement of students depends ultimately on their ability to demonstrate knowledge and ideas in appropriate academic language, both spoken and written. If students are to develop concepts and the language for expressing them, their oral explanations need to be preceded by discussion, reading and note-taking. Written reports and essays are the culmination of a similar process, again involving reading, discussion, note-taking and redrafting.

It is important that classroom learning routines reflect this composite and progressive pattern. Students should have on-going opportunities across the curriculum, to speak and write academic language as they work on a variety of collaborative, interactive tasks. They should discuss, jot down ideas or observations as they occur, transform notes into continuous prose, help each other with redrafting and evaluate their own and one another's work and learn to appreciate what is effective and to check for both linguistic and contextual omissions and errors. They will develop the confidence to tease out new understandings in the familiar, day-to-day language which is immediately available to them, while also acquiring the academic terminology and genres to express academic subject matter accurately. 'A plastic mac keeps the rain off but it stops your sweat getting out' will replaced by 'The plastic used in a plastic mac is impermeable to water and water vapour. It protects from the rain but prevents body vapour from escaping.'

Collaborative learning

Interactive group tasks followed by feedback can provide intensive practice in using new language with a clear purpose. It gives students an opportunity to perform both within the group and to the rest of the class. The setting allows students to use informal, familiar language to discuss work in progress and try out new language. The teacher and more advanced peers can model appropriate academic language in context and as it is needed. Excellent examples of such collaborative language development arise in the preparation for formal group presentations – arguing a point of view for a 'mock' GCSE English oral, for instance, or explaining a design process for a Technology coursework presentation. These occasions give students a clear sense of audience and purpose and an understanding of the need for a relevant academic genre. Listening to other contributions provides language modelling in a meaningful context accompanied by opportunities to compare and discuss appropriate language use. Such presentations could be in the form of written work read aloud or used as a basis for oral explanation thus exemplifying the close link between spoken academic language and written text.

Well-structured collaborative work gives students an understanding of the role of interaction in their own learning – of the purpose of discussion as a basis for the development and final expression of new understandings in both their oral and written work.

Language modelling and clear contextualisation in collaborative presentations help bilingual learners recognise genre distinctions in English that they might otherwise not detect. Beginners in English may find performance in oral presentations daunting, but collaborative preparation can support them and boost their confidence if peers encourage their attempts. Confidence is often increased by using real objects as props and prompts such as single words on a card.

Structuring text

To be comprehensible, both spoken and written text needs structure. Students can develop their structuring skills collaboratively while preparing for formal presentations, as they decide on a running order, sequence sections of text to maximise their impact on the audience and agree on paragraph headings for prompt cards to support oral introductions and summaries. It is much easier to analyse complex processes, whether in Maths, Science, the Humanities, Language or Literature if there is a visual structure or 'key visual'. Oral explanations become better-ordered and more fluent and written analyses clearer and more succinct.

Written text is grammatically more complex than oral language and bound by more rigid formal conventions. It is important that teachers take time to explain and demonstrate new genres. If a new genre is modelled on the board using a pre-set structure it can then be used by students for their own writing. Modelling should be supported by reading the words aloud together with a spoken commentary and talking with the students about the thinking involved. This can give a vivid insight into both the new genre and the writing process itself.

Board modelling can also be a useful format for metalinguistic analysis, for example when modelling a subject-specific genre or in order to demonstrate how grammatical structure or choice of vocabulary can clarify, emphasise or enrich meaning. This is best done informally, in the context of curriculum activities and contextualised examples and in all areas of the curriculum.

Clear text modelling is particularly important for bilingual students. Modelling should be unhurried and the text read out as it is written on the board. Students can complete a printed copy of the same structure – e.g. for recording personal observations of a group Science practical.

By Key Stage 4, students should be able to use a range of genres. For students whose language skills are less advanced and for late-arrivals, teachers can accelerate the progress of their language development by means of various 'scaffolding' techniques: providing paragraph headings, essay plans or writing 'frames' differentiated by the number and length of their sequenced sentence stems. Carefully used, these can provide individually targeted support that can be gradually discarded as students learn to create their own structures.

Such scaffolding, tailored to individual needs and stage of linguistic development, generates confidence and enables bilingual students to communicate understanding they could not express unaided.

Facilitated speaking

Purposeful oral interaction between students and teachers or more fluent peers can operate in pair or small group activities, or as a part of interactive teaching. Discussion which is clearly focused on the task, whether describing a setting or physical process or explaining the concept behind it, provides important opportunities for modelling academic language in a meaningful context. When the teacher and peers are responsive to the interests and level of comprehension of the bilingual students, their learning and language acquisition will be facilitated and they will be encouraged to express personal opinions.

Interaction of this nature gives scope for sensitive differentiation in response to individual interests and comprehension skills and is crucial for bilingual learners. Parents and carers of young children commonly model language for those who are less fluent. Many teachers, and students too, use similar tactics to support bilingual learners by using emphasis, for example, or questions which include possible model answers: 'Is this igneous rock or sedimentary rock?'

Bilingual students often lack the confidence to speak in a large group and do better in pair and small group work. This is especially true of early-stage English learners emerging from the 'silent period'. Collaborative learning also provides opportunity and contextual modelling for expressing personal opinions.

Structured support for facilitated talk can also be given by written or visual cues. Using a key visual such as a chart or flow diagram as a referent for explaining conceptual relationships can guide pupils in the use of the precise, academic language through which the visual is presented. Repetitive practical activities, such as games that invite the repetition of key phrases in a meaningful context are also supportive.

Both these strategies help bilingual learners by providing the repetitive modelling and meaningful language which are mainstays of language acquisition.

Facilitated writing

Students' writing benefits from preparatory discussion to develop ideas and practice and refine the words to express them.

Like talk, academic writing requires purpose and a sense of audience and can also be a means of developing ideas to produce a final text. So students should be taught to make notes and drafts as a precursor to finished work.

Students' written work, like all extended printed text, needs careful structuring and appropriate vocabulary in an appropriate formal genre and this requires some specific teaching. All curriculum subjects should include opportunities to read as well as write academic text. Students' writing should show some independence – passive copying should be restricted to recording already-understood homework instructions, headings or frames to be completed.

Grammatical structure and formal presentation should be taught as it is needed in the context of work in progress.

Conferencing can be helpful for bilingual learners but requires particular sensitivity. Too much correction is disheartening; but they will welcome in-depth explanation of recurring mistakes, such as the omission of the plural 's' (common among speakers of Chinese or Vietnamese languages which do not use the plural form). It is best to focus on students' attempts to express complex concepts and discuss what they meant, listening to their explanations, modelling alternative wording and writing down their ideas in appropriate language, as they warm to the discussion. 'That's really interesting. I think this is what you meant. Would you like to read it and see if I've understood your meaning?'

Progress towards higher levels of academic language

Academic success depends not only on understanding academic subjects but also on the use of appropriate language. Students require a range of specialist subject vocabulary and genres to examine, analyse and make judgements about increasingly complex and abstract concepts. For all students, academic success and the language skills which go with it demand a pedagogy which allows active understanding of new ideas and the language which expresses them and which emphasises critical language skills. Teaching strategies which support bilingual learners will help all students in achieving this.

Implementing change

Homines dum docent discunt
While they teach, men learn
Seneca: *Epistulae Morales*

Teaching is a learning experience and thanks to modern advances in psychology and educational research and continuing academic and political debate on educational issues, teachers are aware that their practice must be flexible – responsive to the needs and aspirations of the students and their academic development. Certain government initiatives, such as the National Literacy and Numeracy Strategies, school policies and teachers' own professional development will require teachers to change and develop. Teachers will need to interpret and assess the pedagogical implications of new ideas and adapt them to the needs of their own students.

When implementing a new teaching strategy teachers have to rely and build on their own knowledge and experience. This requires a degree of trial and error and professional judgement when observing and assessing outcomes. Every curriculum development project must have a clear purpose and an achievable completion date. It should be small scale, short-term and initially restricted to one teaching group. The language involved – spoken and written – should be central. To achieve this the project should be collaborative, involving, for example, partnership with a departmental colleague teaching the same scheme of work to a parallel group, or a support teacher who can share the classroom input. Preparation and evaluation should be fully discussed and recorded, planning notes collaboratively evaluated and redrafted in response to classroom outcomes and written up and shared with staff.

The teacher of the Science lesson described above was already skilled at making herself clearly understood by students, using accessible language and gradually introducing and consolidating new terms. Some of her students were beginning to develop confidence in discussing their work when in pairs or small groups but whole class input, aimed at developing hypotheses and modelling technical language, was dominated by a handful of articulate students. Through one short development project, the teacher was able to change this situation and radically transform whole-class discussion. She adopted two new strategies: the use of board work to give ongoing visual support and a management technique which ensured that all students took part. These strategies became embedded in her teaching repertoire and all her students now have regular opportunities for extensive oral practice to develop their use of academic language and their hypothesising skills, resulting in a marked improvement in their independent writing.

To develop and manage collaborative projects requires timetabled non-contact time for planning and assessment. Embedding them in whole-school development policy ensures that they form a sustained pattern across the curriculum. Students too are central players in pedagogical change. Year 7 students are generally ready to embrace change but they enjoy the confidence-building experience of using familiar skills acquired in primary school, particularly those to do with collaborative learning and independent research. Building on and adapting these to the demands of the various secondary subjects can establish a solid basis for learning and language development in subsequent years.

Where schools have regard for the importance of whole-school curriculum development; where this is well organised, fairly spread and systematically disseminated between colleagues; where it is soundly based on the key principles of relevance and language development, with a view to student empowerment; where these principles have been understood and embraced by all the teachers involved in individual development projects, and they have been empowered to use their own judgement and expertise in responding to the demands of their subject and the perceived needs of the students; where schools have successfully negotiated general acceptance and systematic implementation of such a policy; and where bilingual students are fully included in the mainstream curriculum, students will benefit, standards will rise and teachers will enjoy their teaching more. If the teaching is consistently 'language-aware', students such as Mehmet will shine.

9

Conclusion

Maggie Gravelle

After over thirty years of special funding to raise the achievement of pupils from ethnic minorities, firstly under Section 11 administered by the Home Office and more recently under the Ethnic Minority and Traveller Achievement Grant administered by the Department for Education and Employment, many teachers are still uncertain about the most effective ways of providing the full curriculum entitlement for bilingual learners. There is certainly evidence of good practice. A good many bilingual children achieve great success and there are individual teachers and groups of teachers in specific schools or local education authorities who provide rich and challenging educational experiences for bilingual learners that stimulate learning and assure language development, as the chapters in this book testify.

Nevertheless, under-achievement continues to concern teachers, parents and certain ethnic minority communities. In 1996 Gillborn and Gipps reported on the achievements of ethnic minority pupils as identified by research projects over the previous few years. They found that in general African-Caribbean pupils and more consistently Bangladeshi and Pakistani children achieved less well than their white peers in the early years of education. In secondary schools the trends indicated that children of Indian background attained good grades and that Bangladeshi and African-Caribbean pupils under-achieved.

The Macpherson Report on the Stephen Lawrence Inquiry (1999) has focused attention attention on aspects of institutional racism and in particular exclusions. School policies have been amended to reflect these concerns and to monitor ethnicity in respect of exclusions and sometimes achievement. The Report also recommended that the curriculum be amended in order to value cultural diversity.

The new National Curriculum was already in its late drafts and, despite the Education Secretary's assurances, shows relatively little evidence of taking this recommendation to heart, although the emphasis on inclusion is to be welcomed.

The transfer of Section 11 funding to EMTAG shifted the responsibility from the Home Office to the DfEE. It has also resulted in greater devolvement to schools. It is too early fully to evaluate the effects of this but already some concerns have been expressed about lack of training for teachers, the possible misuse of funds and the trend towards direct classroom support at the expense of advice and training (see Blair and Bourne, 1996, Vance, 2000 and Wiles, 1999). Even before the changes were finalised, bodies such as the 1990 Trust and Race on the Agenda were drawing attention to potential pitfalls in the system. They asked LEAs and governing bodies to consider matters such as support for the bilingual pupils who speak fluent conversational English but whose 'curriculum English' still needs support.

With these changes greater responsibility is being assigned to class teachers and yet the Teacher Training Curriculum issued by the TTA in 1998 made little reference to the need for newly qualified teachers to have the skills, knowledge and understanding to teach students for whom English is not their first language. New guidance has been issued (TTA, 2000) but it does not have statutory status. There is no nationally recognised training route or funding for teachers who specialise in supporting bilingual learners. So there is a danger that instead of raising levels of achievement overall, we will continue to have piecemeal provision with pockets of good practice. It is important, therefore, that we identify what constitutes good practice so that it can be more widely disseminated.

One difficulty is that the National Curriculum requires teachers to assess what children 'know, understand and can do' and as it is always easier to assess skills than knowledge and understanding, this is what teachers, and others, tend to notice and focus on. Such incomplete assessment has aroused concern about bilingual learners in the early stages of acquiring English because their lack of language skills – which are obvious – are assumed to affect their ability to know and understand. Consequently, teachers have focused on what bilingual children cannot do rather than what they can do. They have concentrated on how to remediate the child rather than how to adapt their own pedagogy and curriculum. Teachers need to ask a wholly different set of questions: How do I find out what this child already knows? How do I capitalise on the skills they have? What changes do I need to make to the curriculum in order to make it relevant? How can I organise the classroom and resources to scaffold this child's learning most effectively? What forms of assessment will validate the child's existing skills, knowledge and understanding?

Every teacher plans. Even working within the confines of the increasingly prescriptive curriculums produced by the DfEE and QCA, we need to decide which aspects to tackle, to what depth and with what resources. We need, in other words, to determine the key concepts. What do children most need to learn about this particular topic, subject or area? Frameworks typically provide the medium term planning but the daily detail is determined by individual teachers who know what will be most effective for their class and their children. The contributors to this book demonstrate that by giving attention to certain aspects of planning and particular strategies, the learning and thereby the language development of bilingual pupils will be enhanced without in any way jeopardising the education of the rest of the class. On the contrary, the maxim that 'what is good for bilingual learners is good for all learners' has been convincingly illustrated in these pages.

Building on pupils' experiences

Bilingual learners make up a no more homogenous group than any other set of pupils. Even children who come from similar cultural, linguistic and geographical backgrounds may have little in common. So it is imperative that we get to know pupils as individuals. Information collected and recorded on entry to the school may be the starting point but, as with all our pupils, we will only learn about their aptitudes, interests and attitudes over time and through listening to them.

Several contributors describe the pupils in their classes in terms not just of their ethnic and linguistic backgrounds, important though these are, but also of their previous educational experiences, personalities and attitudes towards schooling or the particular subject. Much of Pilar's progress, for instance was due to her own personality and motivation and these qualities vary from individual to individual, although the teachers' expectations also influence pupils' learning. Blair and Bourne (1998:171) report that the successful schools they studied 'made efforts to connect with the linguistic and cultural background of the children and local community *as part of their educational activity*' (my italics).

Knowing the child's background is not enough – it needs to be actively and purposefully included in the curriculum. Teachers should avoid making assumptions about what children will find familiar and build instead on accurate and precise knowledge of their experiences and environment in selecting suitable texts and other materials.

If the background and skills of the bilingual learners are given a valued place in the curriculum and the teaching, all the children receive positive messages about them. The self-esteem of the bilingual children is raised and this is likely to enhance the extent and rate of their learning. Children's first languages play a significant role in encouraging them to explore ideas and make links between their culture and the curriculum. All pupils benefit from this opportunity to share experiences and extend knowledge. Many young people have similar interests regardless of their ethnic background. On the other hand, racism is a unique experience and it must be challenged through exploring issues sensitively and without confrontation.

The role of the teacher

Teachers clearly have a role in planning a relevant curriculum and should draw on information in their students' profiles. They also have responsibility for extending language and learning through effective organisation and resources.

One aspect of their role is to create a positive and receptive ethos in the classroom. This includes providing a broad range of literature and other material which reflects the backgrounds and interests of all the pupils. Some of this literature should be in languages other than English. Not only can such material extend curricular access but it also demonstrates that English is not the only medium of learning and communication.

Many schools and classrooms have ancilliary and other support staff. The way they are incorporated into the organisation and learning of the classroom sends clear messages about their contribution.

Bilingual adults – teachers, assistants and parents – are invaluable because of their unique pastoral role and the positive models they present to pupils, as well as their knowledge and skills. The attitudes of pupils are influenced by the relationships among the adults they come into contact with and if these are collaborative and respectful the children are more likely to behave similarly.

In order to promote understanding as well as knowledge and skills teachers need to encourage pupils' critical thinking. This can begin in the primary years when children discuss and justify moral judgements and begin to appreciate their complexity. Children's critical and analytical skills continue to develop throughout schooling. If the curriculum is to be truly inclusive, pupils need to be taught to consider variations in points of view and teachers need to provide a climate in which these can be expressed and discussed.

Talk in first language and English

The expression and discussion of views takes place largely through talk, even when discussions are informed by reading and presented in written form. The role of talk, as argued and exemplified by the National Oracy Project, is central to education. And yet the pressure of curriculum content and the emphasis on assessable products appears to be creating classrooms in which exploratory talk is limited. There is a widespread perception among managers, teachers and pupils that discussion is not 'real work'.

All the contributors to this book argue for the importance of talk for children's learning and language development. They acknowledge the place of children's first languages in their cognitive and personal growth as well as in their English language acquisition. But the authors also emphasise that talk needs to be carefully planned and organised in the classroom as part of all children's learning. Talk provides one way of sorting out and confirming one's own ideas and incorporating and testing other people's (see Barnes in Norman, 1992). For bilingual learners it is often the earliest form of communication in English – and the least threatening.

Interaction between pupils takes place largely through talk, which has an important role in forming friendships and introducing classroom routines. Bilingual learners often go through a 'silent period' when they are reluctant to talk but they can still be active listeners.

Teachers are frequently relieved to learn that this 'silent period' is normal and that they do not have to persuade the children to speak. But they still need to make talk accessible to bilingual pupils by providing concrete referents such as pictures, real objects, practical activities and so on. There must be opportunities for pupils to participate and talk when they are ready.

Talk needs to be organised and planned. Children often find small groups an unthreatening way of exploring their ideas. They gain practice and confidence to contribute in larger groups, for example in a whole class brainstorm or discussion. Children need the reassurance that their efforts will be received positively and that teachers are not simply looking for a 'right' answer to a closed question.

Activities which build pupils' confidence in talking are important in developing other language skills, such as writing. Discussion in children's first languages assists their understanding as well as affirming their culture and identity and is likely to take place when there is a real reason for doing so. Writing will often be done in English, although opportunities for translation and for writing in first languages are also supportive and can allow increased access to interesting and challenging activities. Dual language texts and activities can provide a link between home and school and give the parents of bilingual children greater involvement with the curriculum.

Collaborative learning

Not all group work is collaborative. Primary schools have for many years encouraged group work but this can be merely a device for placing children in designated ability groups and giving them similar tasks. Genuine collaborative learning requires participation by all children in an activity that extends and deepens their understanding. Exploratory talk is vital in these situations and can provide opportunities for bilingual learners to make significant and unique contributions. Activities need to be carefully planned so that the process is as important as the product. Edwards and Mercer (1987) distinguish between ritual and principled knowledge. Ritual knowledge is the acquisition of particular routines and drills that may produce the right answers but does not necessarily show understanding, whereas principled knowledge indicates understanding at an explanatory and conceptual level.

Tasks must be designed so that all pupils participate and feel able to contribute their own ideas and knowledge. Young children can find collaboration difficult but, with encouragement, are more likely to question conflicting information and assumptions and to deal with complex issues. A number of strategies facilitate this process: getting pairs of pupils to make a single record, using charts and diagrams as simple ways of recording ideas, re-organising groups so that pupils have to explain and justify their decisions, building from small to larger groups, using practical tasks and concrete materials. Much of the success of collaborative learning depends on planning. Once this is complete teachers can take the role of facilitator and evaluator.

Lunzer and Gardner (1984) developed DARTs (Directed Activities Related to Texts) as ways of helping children to understand texts through deconstruction and reconstruction. Although many of the activities, such as true and false statements, cloze, sequencing and grid completion, can be completed individually their value lies in the accompanying discussion and learning from one another.

From the earliest days children learn as much, if not more, from each other as from their teachers and it is sensible to build on this through collaborative activities. Games involve naturally repetitive language and are informal ways of encouraging collaboration. Elements of competition can be reduced by emphasising the process and the different contribution of all participants. A demanding and challenging goal can often be achieved through sharing tasks. Mixed ability groups provide bilingual learners with a range of language models and enable them to engage with the work at their own cognitive level.

Supportive strategies

Bilingual learners will be successful in a classroom with a positive and supportive ethos in which talk has a central place. Collaborative activities can provide the ideal context for such exploratory talk and this book amply describes such strategies. The best interests of bilingual learners are served by ensuring that the strategies build on their skills, knowledge and understanding and so help them to develop their learning. Learning need not await the development of their English language skills. On the contrary, language development is often contingent upon learning. New concepts provide the ideal context for developing new language.

Non-linguistic support includes the use of pictures, charts, photographs, symbols, maps and diagrams as well as real objects. Illustrations need to be vivid and attractive and enhance the text. Key visuals are more than illustrations. They explain concepts and their relationships. Drama, role-play, games and practical activities can all convey ideas, at least in part, by non-linguistic means and so help bilingual learners to understand and participate. Teachers need to be alert to the possibility that some of these activities may be culturally specific. British children, for example, are accustomed to maps of the world which place Europe at the centre. Pupils from a different educational background may be more familiar with different orientations.

Bilingual assistants offer the potential for great support but are often used in limited ways. Their insights should help children beyond the early stages of acquiring English, and their skills extend beyond translation and interpreting. They are an important link between home and school and can also offer guidance on the selection and use of resources.

The place of talk as a supportive strategy includes the use of repetition, prediction and rehearsal before and during reading, and recapping and retelling afterwards. Brainstorming enables pupils not only to share their ideas but also reminds them of the discussion. They might then want to re-organise suggestions as a precursor to writing. If talk is to lead to writing, teachers need to structure the discussion appropriately. By using substitution tables bilingual pupils can achieve a piece of writing which is conceptually challenging but linguistically attainable. In some ways substitution tables can be said to be versions of writing frames, although because they offer a more limited range of alternatives they are particularly suitable for early stage bilingual learners. Pupils move on to the support of writing frames and story planners, although as Lewis and Wray (1995) insist, these need to be flexible and temporary.

Language does not simply consist of a string of words. Merely explaining or translating key vocabulary is inadequate. Words are organised into particular structures and are set in contexts that give them meaning That is one of the reasons why it is vital that bilingual learners are part of the context in which language is being used for real purposes of learning and interaction – the classroom.

Progression and assessment

Planning is important in order to track progression and assess achievement. Our medium term planning indicates the direction and rate of progression, and the details of daily plans should include ways in which we will assess children's achievements along the route.

Progress is rarely uniform. Children will sometimes confound us by appearing to have forgotten something which we were sure they understood, or at other times by taking great strides forward. This is partly because teachers and curriculum planners have a particular view of achievement and progress which is not necessarily matched by every child. Pupils bring a variety of experiences from their homes or earlier schooling to the classroom. Some will have been in formal educational settings where creative writing or personal opinion was not valued. Eve Gregory (1996) describes a five year-old boy of Chinese background whose experiences of literacy and the value placed upon it at home made him reluctant to participate in some of the 'frivolous' literacy activities of school, where children who could not yet read were encouraged to browse through books and take them home to share with their parents. Others will be frustrated if their understanding and achievements are not recognised because they do not yet have the skills to express them in English.

Many bilingual learners have highly developed metalinguistic skills. Any assessments made of bilingual children should acknowledge these skills and, since oral fluency often precedes the ability to express oneself in writing, talk needs to be highly valued. Both talk and writing are necessary to confirm understanding and to provide clear models of appropriate language use. As children move into writing, their progress must be well supported. Writing is not simply speech on the page and the differences between the two forms of communication should be made clear. The development of literacy does not need to await complete oral fluency but should go on simultaneously, as the learning demands.

Children do not learn everything we teach, nor is their learning confined to our teaching. But thoughtful planning is more likely to ensure the relevance of what we teach.

Bilingual staff are invaluable in assessing children's learning. They can reduce the risk that children will be misdiagnosed as having special educational needs when their level of achievement is due to a specific concept gap which can be closed quickly with appropriate support. Accurate assessment is vital and so too is support beyond the initial stages. It is easy enough to identify what bilingual children cannot do but more difficult to meet their need for academic language development. Additional support must be carefully targeted and sufficiently flexible to respond to changing circumstances. When additional support is not available it is even more vital that teachers plan in ways which will enable bilingual pupils to get their full curriculum entitlement.

Planning takes place on several levels. Teachers need an overview of the curriculum in order to plan with children's existing knowledge, skills and understanding in mind. They will be guided and influenced also by the National Curriculum, other government initiatives and examination syllabuses. The progression and continuity needs to be made clear to pupils and their families so that they know what route is being taken and where and how they will reach their destination.

On a more detailed, day-to-day level teachers need to build on what they know about their pupils' knowledge and skills as well as the specific demands of the learning. They need to consider learning in its widest sense, as social, cognitive and linguistic. In taking such a broad and holistic view of the learning process they will be able to plan the most appropriate support for the children in their classrooms.

Bibliography

Barnes, D, Britton, J and Rosen, H (1971, 2nd edition 1986) *Language, the learner and the school*, Penguin

Barnes, D (1976) *From communication to curriculum*, Penguin

Barnes, D. (1992) The Role of Talk in Learning in Norman, K. (ed) *Thinking Voices*, Hodder and Stoughton

Blair, M and Bourne, J (1998) *Making the Difference: Teaching and learning strategies in successful multi-ethnic schools*, Open University and DfEE

Bourne, J and McPake, J (1991) *Partnership Teaching*, London, NFER/DES

Collier, V (1989) How Long? A Synthesis of Research on Academic Achievement in a Second Language, *TESOL Quarterly*, Vol 23 No 3

Collier, V and Thomas, W (1999) Making US schools effective for English language learners, *TESOL Matters* Vol 9 nos 4,5,6

Cummins, J (1984) *Bilingualism and Special Education: issues in assessment and pedagogy*, Multilingual Matters.

Cummins, J (1996) *Negotiating Identities; education for empowerment in a diverse society*, California Association for Bilingual Education

DES (1975) *A Language for Life* (The Bullock Report) HMSO

DfEE (1998) *The National Literacy Strategy; Framework for Teaching*, DfEE

Dulay, H., Burt, M and Krashen, S (1982) *Language Two*, Oxford University Press

Edwards, D and Mercer, N (1987) *Common Knowledge; the development of understanding in the classroom*, Methuen

Edwards, V (1998) *The Power of Babel*, Trentham

Gillborn, D and Gipps, C (1996) *Recent Research on the Achievements of Ethnic Minority Pupils*, HMSO

Gravelle, M (1996) *Supporting Bilingual Learners in Schools*, Trentham

Gregory, E (1996) *Making Sense of a New World*, Paul Chapman

Hart, S (1996) *Beyond Special Needs: Enhancing children's learning through innovative thinking,* Paul Chapman

Jones, R (1999) *Teaching racism or tackling it? – multicultural stories from white beginning teachers.* Trentham

Levine, J (1996) Developing Pedagogies for Multilingual Classes in Meek, M (ed) *Developing Pedagogies in the Multilingual Classroom; the writings of Josie Levine*, Trentham

Lewis, M and Wray, D (1995) *Developing Children's Non-fiction Writing; working with writing frames*, Scholastic

Lunzer, E and Gardner, K (1984) *Learning from the written word*, Oliver and Boyd

MacNamara, S and Moreton, J (1995) *Changing Behaviour; teaching children with emotional and behavioural difficulties in primary and secondary classrooms*, David Fulton

Macpherson Report (1999) *The Stephen Lawrence Inquiry: Report of an Inquiry by Sir William Macpherson*, Stationery Office

Mohan, B (1986) *Language and Content,* Reading, Mass., Addison Wesley

Ovando, C and Collier, V (1998) *Bilingual and ESL classrooms: Teaching in multicultural contexts*, McGraw Hill

Philips, T (1985) *Beyond Lip Service in* Wells, G and Nicholls, J (eds) *Language and Learning; an interactional perspective*, Falmer Press

Savva, H (1990) The rights of bilingual children in Carter, R (ed) *Knowledge about Language and the Curriculum,* Hodder and Stoughton

Smith, F (1978) *Reading,* Cambridge University Press

Teacher Training Agency (1998) *Teaching: High Status, High Standards*, Circular 4/98, DfEE

Teacher Training Agency, (2000) *Raising the Attainment of Minority Ethnic Pupils*, TTA

Vance, M (2000) Key issues for education – one year on, in *Multicultural Teaching* Vol 18 No 2

Vasquez, M (1996) Integrating a Small Group of ESL Students into Mainstream Science; partnership teaching in Clegg, J *Mainstreaming ESL; case studies in integrating ESL students into the mainstream curriculum*, Multilingual Matters

Wiles, S (1999) Evaluating Additional Grant Funding for Minority Ethnic Pupils in *EAL and Bilingualism: Policies for a New Agenda*, NALDIC

Wong Fillmore, L (1991) Second-language learning in children; a model of language learning in social context in Bialystock, E (ed) *Language Processing in Bilingual Children,* Cambridge University Press

Index